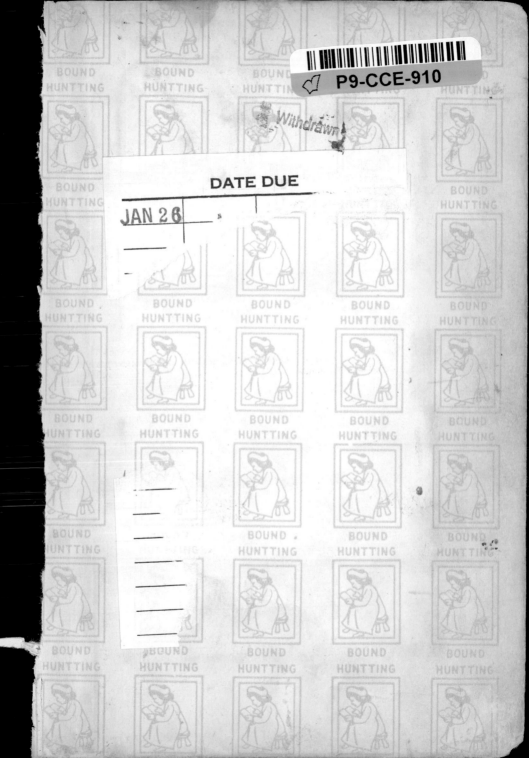

DAVID FARRAGUT
Sea Fighter

DAVID FARRAGUT

Sea Fighter

by Marie Mudra

Decorations by Douglas Gorsline

JULIAN MESSNER, INC., NEW YORK

Published by Julian Messner, Inc.
8 West 40th Street, New York 18

*Published Simultaneously in Canada
By The Copp Clark Company, Ltd.*

Copyright 1953, by Marie Mudra
Printed in the United States of America

Third Printing, 1961

Library of Congress Catalog Card No. 53-10510

This book is affectionately dedicated
to my husband
Dr. James Mudra

Contents

Contents

DAVID FARRAGUT
Sea Fighter

1

Log Cabin at Stony Point—1806

Lıttle James Glasgow Farragut squirmed and shifted on the hot limestone rock, watching his brother Will, sitting cross-legged across from him, sorting out scraps of deerskin.

Glasgow—his family called him that rather than by his first name—could no longer remain quiet. The rough rock scratched and burned through the seat of his pants. "Will," he said, standing up, "I'm going to climb the poplar. I'll watch for Papa. Maybe I'll see some Indians." From there he would see the road winding down to meet the highway at the foot of the hill.

"Stay here," Will said. "Watch how I make this sling. It's time you learned to sling a shot."

Glasgow grumbled. Just because Will was nine years old he thought he knew everything! The younger boy would much rather be up in the tall poplar looking across the Holston River to Stony

Point, Tennessee, where he would see their father's ferryboat at its little wharf.

But even talk of Indians could not distract Will today. "Sit down, brother," he said, and his tone meant it. So Glasgow sat. He watched Will take his knife and slit a strip from the scraps of deerskin before him, the knife sparking as it struck the stone.

"See," Will said as he stretched the thong and measured it for length and thickness, "they must be the same size." Then he took a narrow oblong strap of leather. "Now—knot one cord through this hole on the small side, and another through the hole opposite. There's your sling!" He held it up.

"Let's try her out, Glasgow," Will said as he selected a smooth round pebble from the pile beside him. "See, put it into this oblong pocket." With two ends of the cord in his right hand he gave the sling a few pulls, and both boys got up. "Watch that little sugar maple down there. I'm aiming to hit it."

Setting himself, he whirled the sling around his head, then let loose of one of the cords with a snap. Two hundred feet downhill the top maple leaves trembled from the impact of the shot, and Will proudly slapped his leg as he passed the sling to his brother. "Here, you try. Now that you're five you must learn to slingshot, too. Aim for that young walnut tree there. That's a full one-hundred-foot target."

Glasgow gave the sling a few clumsy twirls above his head; it slipped, the pebble bouncing weakly to the rock beneath and skittering off into the blackberry bushes. He felt ashamed. "I can't seem to let it go."

Will handed him more pebbles from the pile. "Try again. Learn to snap it and let go at the same time."

Glasgow puffed with effort. On the sixth throw the pebble flew off sideways down the slope.

"That's better. Go on, try some more," Will said as he sat down to make two more slings, because he had heard the story of the sling many times before. Their father, Major George Farragut, was born on the island of Minorca in the Mediterranean Sea, and every man there had to be an expert slinger. Warriors always went to battle with three slings, one around the neck, one hanging at the waist, the third in the hand ready to use.

"I hit it! I hit it!" Glasgow jumped up and down. "Did you see that, Will?" Tattered tips of thin leaves fluttered below.

"You wouldn't get much breakfast that way," Will laughed. "But it's pretty good."

He knew Will was referring to a story the Major had told them. The Minorcans hung a basket of fruit in a pomegranate tree and not a piece of fruit could their father have until he shot the whole basket down. Will could do it; now Glasgow had to learn to do as well. But he was tired. He had had enough for today.

Will stuffed the leftover deerskin into a pouch in his linsey shirt as their dog, Skipper, scrambled onto the rock between them. "How did you get here, boy?" Will demanded.

"Maybe he's come to tell us it's most time for supper," Glasgow suggested hopefully. "Nancy said we'll have honey cake for dessert."

Their sister, Nancy, the only Farragut with blond hair, was older than Glasgow and liked to boss him sometimes. The day before, they had found some wild honey in an old hollow oak, far past the woods beyond the cow pasture. Mother had scolded them for going so far from home when their father was away. But when Glasgow told her about the honey she gave him a bowl to fetch it, and warned, "Make fast about it and be careful."

Early that morning Major Farragut had gone to Knoxville to buy tea and sugar which had just come from Virginia, and he had promised to bring them a surprise the next day. It was the month of July, 1806, and the Cherokees were on the warpath again because they hated the white man's treaty made the past fall. Only the week before, Merrill Brady had spent a night with the Farraguts and told how a neighbor had been found dead beside his plow, killed by the Indians. The boys now knew well why their father had ordered, "Stay where you can hear your mother call."

Skipper lay between the boys while Glasgow rubbed his ear and Will rested his head on the soft furry body. "Mama's probably going to wait till dark for supper, in case Pa does get back today," Glasgow said, gazing across the river.

Skipper jerked one ear high, springing up to stand at the end of the rock, listening, while Will, alarmed, jumped up to peer into the valley. "Maybe that's Pa now," he said. But to be on guard he grabbed Skipper around the neck. "Down. Be quiet now!"

The boys saw two horsemen trotting past the evergreens down below. "There's Pa on Black Bess," Will said, relieved but excited, "and he's got someone with him."

"Let's give him a surprise," said Glasgow, flattening himself on the rock hidden by the blackberry bushes. His brother did likewise, holding the dog, and they watched the two men coming up the hill on the dirt road leading to their farm.

"Well, John," they heard the Major say, "we've made it, just in time for supper." The horses were climbing slowly.

Suddenly the boys leaped out, waving their arms wildly, screaming Indian whoops and yells, while Skipper barked sharply and danced about Black Bess.

"Git, you heathens, git!" their father cried, pretending to defend himself. The brothers laughed, hearing him say, "They're my boys, Colonel—as quiet as a bunch of wharf hands with a broken barrel of snuff."

The boys ran on ahead to tell their mother the news.

As Glasgow trotted along he thought of his father. He had been a lieutenant in the state navy of South Carolina, and during the Revolutionary War had built many galleys at Charleston which had harried the big British fleet patrolling the seaboard. While he was commanding one of these vessels, on a mission from Philadelphia to Charleston aboard an American privateer, his arm had been shattered by a cannon ball and he was captured by the British who had taken Charleston in 1780. Ever since then Father's arm had bothered him in rainy weather; so at house raisings and log rollings he directed the building while his companions swung the axes to fell the trees and did the other manual work.

When the boys were approaching their home, Glasgow recalled the story. At first the Farragut log cabin built by his father had been one large room; but as the family grew, wings were added on each side. A covered walk joined the central room to a summer kitchen set some distance from the house. A barn and chicken pens lay still farther to the rear, and a cow pasture beyond.

Smoke curled lazily from the chimney of his home, and Glasgow knew supper had been ready a long time. It was only being kept hot. When things were cooking, the smoke came up fast in big puffs.

A snake fence closed in the large yard, and the land around the house was all cleared so that no prowling Indian could hide there undetected.

The brothers tried to pull up the sagging crossbar gate after the riders; but it raised yellow dust as they dragged it, and their father dismounted to help them.

As they went on he said, "You will be very welcome under our roof, John. My wife often has said you haven't been down this way much since we left Knoxville."

"A good sign, isn't it?" said Colonel McKee.

Even little Glasgow knew what he meant. Where John McKee was, the Indians would be causing trouble. He was helping the government arrange a settlement with the Choctaws, whose lands lay far south of the Cherokees in lower Mississippi Territory. Chief Doublehead of the Cherokees had given Choctaw land to the United States without the Choctaws' permission and they thought they were being cheated. Colonel McKee had to make peace between the two tribes and his United States.

The boys ran into the house to announce the visitor; and Mrs. Farragut came to the door, hands outstretched in greeting. "What a pleasure and a surprise!" she said, smiling.

Colonel McKee, pressing his coonskin cap over his heart, bowed from the waist, and then took both her hands in his big grasp.

Both men wore the common buckskins and moccasins; but Mrs. Farragut was dressed in a full-flowing homespun dress, a cap with a broad brim of white outlining her face.

"I trust you saw some of our old friends in Knoxville," she said as she went into the house before them. "Are many of them gone?"

"There are many newcomers since our day, but all the old-timers stay on. The place has grown since you lived there," said the Colonel.

In the house she turned to present the children. "You remember William, our eldest, Colonel. He was learning to walk when you saw him last in Knoxville.

Will thought he was almost a man, and hated to be reminded of his baby years; so Glasgow understood why he jumped when Father said, "Unsaddle the horses, Will."

"And this is Glasgow, our first-born at Stony Point," Mrs. Farragut continued.

The smaller boy stepped forward to shake hands.

As their mother introduced Nancy, Glasgow watched her smooth her skirts, her blond pigtails resting on her shoulders. She dropped a pretty curtsy to the Colonel. "How wonderful she is," he thought, "keeping her eyes down so prim and proper! No one would guess she is really a tomboy."

On the wall beside the empty fireplace was a large peg where Major Farragut hung his saddlebags.

"What's in them? What did you bring us?" asked Nancy all in one breath.

"Tea and a few little things," her father chuckled, "but you cannot see them until we've had a bite to eat."

Laying his gun across the large deer antlers above the mantel, he said, "Young Merrill Brady is bringing your sugar tomorrow, Mrs. Farragut. Brady has agreed to stay with us for the rest of the summer and fall."

"Good! He will be a great help in the busy season on our farm."

"Come, John, let's get the dust off us." Major Farragut turned to his friend. Taking towels, the two men went out to the well at the back of the house.

"Mama, Mama!" cried Nancy. "George Antoine is on the chair near the table, getting his fingers in the honey cake!"

"Put him in his own little chair, Nancy." Hurrying to the kitchen, Mrs. Farragut called, "Gentlemen, don't be too long. Supper's most ready." Then again to Nancy, "Come, dear, set another place."

The children waited until their father and the Colonel sat down at the large trestle table, made of walnut and polished to a rich brown. Then they seated themselves, comfortable in the candles' glow, Nancy next to McKee on one side, and Will and Glasgow opposite them. Baby George sat next to his mother at one end, in his own little hickory armchair with a cowhide bottom. The Major sat at the head of the table.

A large hot Brunswick pie was placed before their father; and as each one passed his plate, the Major handed along a fine serving of squirrel meat, rich brown gravy, and some delicious crust. Mrs. Farragut added a large helping of dark red ham with its sweet rim of fat flavored with brown sugar and cloves. Then she gave each a slice of hoecake—made of water-ground meal—into which was pressed a generous portion of butter from the golden mound in the blue dish near her.

There was buttermilk with fat pieces of butter floating in it, sweet milk with heavy cream for those who liked it; black-eyed peas, fresh corn on the cob, and cabbage; and maple syrup for sweetening!

As the eating slowed down, conversation began; and Will, who liked stories about Indians, asked Colonel McKee, "Will there be more fighting, sir?"

"Hush, Will. Let's hope that's done for now," admonished his mother.

But the men kept on talking about Chief Doublehead. He was saving a piece of land for himself in his last treaty between the Cherokees and the white man; and another native—Chief Bonepolisher—did not like it, which might cause trouble between them and the Americans.

Glasgow considered tales of the sea, which he had never seen, much more exciting, and paid little heed to the conversation. Instead he eyed a juicy piece of squirrel meat in the pie and, the first chance he had to interrupt, he asked, "Can I have that little piece of meat, Pa?"

"Save room for the honey cake, brother," Nancy whispered audibly, and Father smiled.

Mrs. Farragut began removing the dishes, setting them on the low cupboard behind her, with Nancy helping. Now she brought the yellow cake in its golden honey, cutting big pieces with long golden strings of honey dripping onto each dish. Glasgow thought nothing in the whole world tasted better than honey cake, and creamy milk to go with it.

"Will that hold you till breakfast, son?" his father asked, while the Colonel chuckled. Glasgow could barely nod his head after that last bite of cake.

Supper over, the men settled down for a smoke. Mrs. Farragut moved the candles to the mantelpiece at the other side of the room. Then she went to put sleepy little George Antoine to bed while Nancy, and the boys for once, cleared away the dessert dishes without being told. They were anxious to see what was in the saddlebags.

But they had to wait until Mrs. Farragut was seated in her own special chair—a roughhewn hickory rocker. Then their father knocked the ashes from his corncob pipe and placed it on the mantel. Finally he took down the saddlebags. Out came boxes of tea and bags of green coffee beans. Nancy kept skipping about, eager to see better. Will tried to act as if he didn't care; and Glasgow tried to imitate Will, but his hazel eyes followed every move his father made.

"Well, Miss," Major Farragut said, "yours is the first present."

Nancy excitedly untied the ribbons of a tiny package and pulled out a small silver object from a cherry-red flannel bag. She gasped and then squealed with delight, "A thimble!"—slipping it onto her middle finger as she had seen her mother do. "Oh, Papa, it's lovely!" she cried, jumping up to pull his head down for a kiss and a hug.

"A bit loose now," her father said, smiling at her pleasure, "but you'll soon grow into it."

Next he presented Mrs. Farragut with some needles and small steel sewing scissors. He gave Will a little knife, showing him how to open the two steel blades that were folded inside.

Glasgow could scarcely stand still. Had his father forgotten him? He stood on tiptoe, waiting his turn, and at last the Major handed him a large oblong package wrapped round and round with paper. Twice the boy dropped it before he got all the paper off. It was a book! And when he opened the brown leather cover he found it to be an illustrated volume about sailing ships! Glasgow hugged it to him tightly. "Oh, Pa!" he began, then threw himself on the bearskin rug and was lost in the book. Now he could see what his beloved ships really looked like!

"Takes after you, Major," Colonel McKee remarked, "liking the sea so well, even when he's never seen it."

"He'll see it someday," Glasgow heard his father say. He wondered when that day would come—when he could see a real sailing vessel, not just the ferryboat his father kept down at Stony Point.

Will soon tired of trying out his new knife on a piece of kindling wood, but Glasgow was still studying eagerly the illustrated vessels when their mother called, "Children, it's time for bed."

Taking candles from a small peg-leg table beside her, she gave one to Will and Glasgow and another to Nancy. "Good night, Colonel McKee." The children chorused their good night's, too.

As the boys settled in their beds they heard their father say, "When will you be back, John?"

"If all is well, within a fortnight."

2

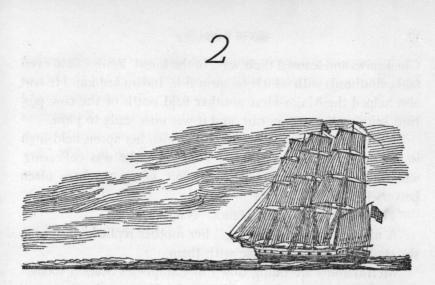

Glasgow Acts as Scout

Augusт brought hot, dry weather, and only the corn in the bottom lands along the river was growing well. More and more the Major kept looking up at the unbroken blue sky for signs of rain; but even the Great Smoky Mountains were clear in the distance, though the Indians had named them so because the mist, shifting about their peaks, made them look as though they were smoking.

Now the Major walked to the barn, where Glasgow was getting a lesson in milking from Merrill Brady. "That's it, boy. Steady tugs on old Minorca," he said.

It was good to have young Brady to help, for the boys thought there wasn't a thing in the world that he could not do. Merrill knew how to track game, how to step through the woods without crackling twigs underfoot. Once he had lived with some friendly

11

Chickasaws and learned their ways in the forest. Brady could even make flintheads with which to spear fish, Indian-fashion. He had also helped the Major clear another field north of the cow pasture, burning the stumps out, and it was now ready to plow.

Mrs. Farragut came toward the barn with her apron held high in her hand, making a basket for the eggs she was collecting, while Nancy brought eggs from the loft, where the hens often perversely laid them.

"That's all I could find, Mama," Nancy said.

"A nice lot for one morning," her mother replied, smiling as she started toward the house with them.

"Merrill and I are riding down to Campbell's Station today," the Major said guardedly, "and John McKee may be there and come back with us. Will you make out all right without us?"

"We'll manage," Mrs. Farragut nodded. "The boys are going to pick cherries for me, so Nancy and I can get some preserving done this afternoon."

Glasgow watched young Brady finish milking, and saw Will take Minorca down through the pasture gate to her calf; then he carried the milk pail to the kitchen. His father and Brady were saddling their horses and checking their rifles and powder horns.

"We won't be long," said the Major with forced cheerfulness as he mounted the mare. "Be back by the middle of the afternoon probably."

Glasgow knew that his father had been watching for Colonel McKee anxiously for days, and sensed that trouble was brewing; but he shrugged away the ominous feeling as he went to help Will pick cherries.

Shortly after noon he and Nancy and Will had finished pitting the cherries and Glasgow went to the well to wash the sticky juice from his purple fingers. It was hot in the kitchen, but cool outdoors. "Will," he called, "I'm going to the big rock. Come on down."

Skipper saw him go and followed, panting eagerly.

"Don't go farther than the rock," warned his mother as she churned the morning's milk in an open crock.

He climbed up on the big rock and soon was high in the poplar tree that grew beside it. It looked like maybe it would rain today, he decided, for the leaves were turning their silver sides to the wind. Now as always Glasgow imagined he was in the rigging of a ship's mast. The wind rustling the leaves made them sound like ocean waves, his father had told him. After a while he slid down to the rock and lay beside Skipper, dozing in the cool shade of the tree.

Something woke him and he sensed danger. Skipper was standing alert, his hair bristling. Glasgow eased himself up, crouching to see what the dog saw. Skipper started to growl; but Glasgow spoke tensely, though softly. "Quiet, Skip. Down!"

"If Will would only come!" he thought.

Then among the thick evergreens along the river road he saw Indians, their copper skins gleaming in the sun. Would they come up the hill? No—they had turned off toward the wharf where Major Farragut kept his ferryboat.

Not waiting to see what they would do next, Glasgow ran, crouching, through the tall dry grass, Skipper trotting with him to the farm. Slipping under the sagging gate, the boy crept around to the kitchen behind the house. Stumbling through the door, he gasped, "Indians!"

Will and Nancy froze like statues. His mother held the long iron preserving spoon in mid-air. "Indians?"

"Down by the ferry," Glasgow continued breathlessly. "Don't know if they're coming up here."

Mrs. Farragut ran out and grabbed baby George Antoine from the yard, then pushed him into Will's hands as she ordered the children up the ladder to the loft above the kitchen. She shut the door and slipped the bar into place, then closed the shutter

on the window and barred it. Next she smothered the fire logs
with ashes, and Glasgow, watching, knew why: smoke coming
out the chimney would show the Indians that someone was in
the summer kitchen.

"Will, come down," she called. The children were peering
down at her from the loft. She warned them now, "Don't any of
you make a sound, no matter what you hear. Will, bar the door
after me when I go outside; then return to the loft. Pull the
ladder up and shut the trap door. And remember, not a sound."

It was a long, long time for the children to stay quiet among
the stored potatoes and apple barrels, afraid to breathe in the
dark, not knowing what would happen next.

Then, after what seemed hours of tortured waiting, they heard
the welcome voices of their mother and father below, and
tumbled down the ladder. They were all talking at once and it
took several minutes for the children to quiet down enough to
hear what had occurred.

After leaving the summer kitchen their mother had run swiftly
across to the big house, where she shut and latched all the windows and the back door. Seizing an ax, she had opened the front
door a crack.

One Indian was at the yard gate, and when he saw her he leaped
over it with a howl and ran toward the house. Slamming the
door, she pushed the iron bar with its chain into place, hearing
the whoops of the other Indians racing toward her across the
yard.

Soon they were pounding on the wooden door, and one
ordered in English, "Let us come in!" The others were shouting
in Indian, but Mrs. Farragut could not make out any Cherokee
words.

"Who are you and where are you from?" she called out to gain
time, hoping her husband and Merrill Brady might arrive.

She heard them shuffling about, grunting, chattering. "More talk later," said the one in English. "Nice lady, open door," he begged.

"Nolichucky Jack won't like this. I'll tell him," she warned. That was the name the Indians gave John Sevier, Governor of Tennessee and famous Indian fighter, known and feared by all of them. "Nolichucky Jack won't like it," she repeated. "Go away."

Grunts and loud outbursts followed, and she continued to hear their moccasined feet padding on the clay earth around the front of the house.

"Give us firewater, we go away. Indians need firewater. Long journey," pleaded the Indian in English.

Elizabeth Farragut did not approve of whisky for anybody, and certainly not for Indians; but if giving it to them would save her children, she would do so. She considered a moment, and then decided. "I'll give you all the firewater I have if you will go away."

"Nice lady," the spokesman answered; then he muttered something to the other Indians, and everything was quiet outside.

She hesitated, suspecting a trick; but the desperate situation required taking a chance. "Step back from the door; I'll put the jug out," she said. She waited, hearing them shuffling away from the door, then put her ear against it to detect any sounds. There were none; so she carefully slipped the iron bar from the bolt, opened the door, and pushed the brown jug with her foot quickly through the crack.

A knife whizzed through the air, embedding itself in the heavy wooden door just as she slammed it shut. She had been quicker than the Indian, and he yelled in rage as he threw himself against it. After Mrs. Farragut had slid the bar into position, leaning breathless against the wall but determinedly clutching the handle of her ax, she called out she would use it on the first neck that showed itself in the house.

No one answered, and she heard the gurglings as the Indians passed the jug around; so she knew they had forgotten her temporarily. Now a new sound of running feet arose; excited gabbling followed, and more running feet fading out quickly. Could the Indians be gone, taking some sudden alarm? Or was it a trick? Weakly she leaned against the wall, waiting.

After a long time she heard horses' hoofs and then the Major's loud "Hallo! Hallo!"

She threw open the door and ran to his arms, then broke away quickly to say, "We must let the children out." The Major had followed his wife to the kitchen.

Glasgow knew he would never forget how his father looked that day with, as his mother put it, "his Spanish blood boiling."

"Who was it?" the Major shouted, his eyes flashing. "Was it Bonepolisher and his Cherokee rebels?"

"I don't know," Mrs. Farragut answered. "They might have been the Shawnees from the north or the Creeks from the south, but I am certain they were not Cherokees."

"We met John McKee at Campbell's Station. He is so sure the Cherokees promise no trouble that he's gone on to Choctaw country. But they may come back," added the Major grimly. "The throwing of that knife shows the ugly frame of mind they're in. You know, if they come, what may happen."

Will and Glasgow had heard the tales of Indian massacres often and they knew what could happen if these redmen returned. Gun in hand, the Major was halfway to the door when Mrs. Farragut's voice stopped him.

"George, don't rush out alone," she begged. "If you must go after them, collect some of your militia company. You'll need a dozen or more to be a match for the Indians."

As the Major of his band of mounted militia, Farragut had to protect the exposed frontier settlements against attacks. Now, muttering at the delay, he took his militia uniform out of the sea chest where it had lain for some time, fading and tarnishing. Glasgow and Will had never seen him in uniform before and to them his blue and red trimmings were still bright. Their father mounted on his horse, with saber at his belt, was a splendid sight to them. He rode off in a cloud of dust, the white horsehair from his tall dragoon hat streaming high above him.

Mrs. Farragut set Will to splitting kindling on the block near the kitchen, while Nancy and Glasgow helped her finish the preserving. Busy at their homey tasks, they forgot their fears for a while. Then they heard a pattering on the roof, and Will came running in as the long-looked-for summer rain fell. "Pa will be glad of this!" he shouted.

They all stood in the doorway watching the downpour, breathing in the cool, moist air as hungrily as the earth and the leaves drank in the water. Near suppertime the rain wore down to a drizzle. The Major came home, then, wet clear through and his anger somewhat dampened, too. He and his men had almost overtaken the Indians three miles above Stony Point, catching sight of them on the other side of the Holston River in canoes left there earlier. The militia managed to kick up the water about the canoes, and the gunfire made the Indians realize that the Holston settlement was well guarded.

"They won't show themselves around here again," said the Major. "By the time we could get the ferry across, the rain would wipe out their trail; but they've had their warning."

"Come, come, we've had enough of Indians for one day," Mrs. Farragut said as they gathered around the supper table; and in a Prayer before Grace they gave thanks that they were once more together, safe and sound.

3

Voyage by Flatboat

Glasgow saw snow come early that fall of 1806, and his father coaxed Merrill Brady into staying on until spring. During the long, cold winter the Major and Brady often went down to Campbell's Station to keep abreast of the news; and there they heard much talk about the new Louisiana Territory, purchased by the United States three years before.

Some of the men from the Station had already traveled to the area to see it for themselves, and brought back glowing reports about "the meadowland that stretches for a thousand miles along the Mississippi River." At the mouth of the river lay the rich city of New Orleans, where their old friend and neighbor, William Claiborne, had been appointed by President Jefferson to govern the lower half of this new territory.

Glasgow also heard his father relate the story of the arrest of Aaron Burr, the Vice-President of the United States, for treason. Mr. Burr had plotted to set up a new empire in the Louisiana Territory and be its emperor!

One evening in March the Major came home with stories of the elegant French and Spanish in New Orleans, and the fine living they had down there. "Just think! There's a cathedral, and a square before it where the military drills and parades are held. The brick houses of the city are covered with whitewashed plaster and have bright tile roofs like my family home in Minorca."

Glasgow knew something special must have happened to make his father so excited, and he watched his mother as she rocked to and fro in her low hickory rocking chair. After listening quietly she asked, "George, why are you talking about all this?"

The Major blurted it out at once. "Here," and he handed her a crisp thick paper. "Governor Claiborne has offered me a commission as sailing master in the American Navy. He's asked me to bring my family to New Orleans to live."

Her chair stopped with a jerk. Leave this home and her friends? What would she, a country girl, do in such an elegant city as New Orleans?

"Elizabeth," her husband's voice pleaded, "think what it would mean to me to feel a rolling deck beneath my feet again, the smell of salt air in my lungs! I could complete my life as I began it in my new homeland—in the service of the American Navy."

Elizabeth knew that he was thinking of the first time he set foot in America, when he brought his ship to port from Havana to New Orleans.

"To return to my first home, my dear," he continued. "With my family. Of course, I wouldn't do it without your consent."

• "I understand what this chance means to you," she smiled.

"And though I'm born and bred in the country, and can't see myself living in the city, if it's life in the Navy you want, so be it. We shall go."

"Yippee! Yippee!" Glasgow pounded the table excitedly. "Now I'll see real ships and sail them, too!"

"Mind your manners, son," his mother admonished gently.

"You won't be sorry, Elizabeth," the Major said. "Now, Merrill"—turning to young Brady who had been listening to this conversation—"you will have to help. I'll probably have to go down to New Orleans in the spring, and you will bring my family down by boat later on."

"You can depend on me, sir," young Brady said eagerly. "I've never made the trip, Major, and I'd like to see that city once."

Nancy and Will ran in and heard the news, Will remaining strangely silent.

Nancy cried, "New Orleans? Tell me more, Papa."

"Well, Miss, in that elegant city little girls always remember they are young ladies. They dress in silks and laces."

Nancy would like the silks and laces, Glasgow thought, but she would not be able to follow Will and him everywhere or climb trees.

The Major continued, "Long before your brothers become sailors, you will learn to trip and mince like all the other city girls. You may go to the convent school of the Ursuline sisters. They will make a perfect lady out of you, even teach you how to sew a fine seam."

"Where can we learn to sail?" asked Glasgow.

"On the big lake behind New Orleans, and the river beside it will give you all the sailing you want." The Major leaned forward, explaining, "You know, boys, a great levee holds the Mississippi River back, otherwise the city itself would be under water."

Will still had said nothing. "Son," his father addressed him, "there are many, many soldiers there. In the beautiful Place d'Armes before the cathedral they have splendid drills each Sunday."

Will, who had been sitting with lowered head, now raised it. "I just don't like leaving Stony Point, Papa"—and suddenly he left the table. At the door he turned. "I *like* it here." And then he ran outside.

Mrs. Farragut took her cloak from the peg and went after him, Glasgow following her to the door. He saw Will leaning against the kitchen door, head down, kicking at the hard earth with his moccasins. By that he knew his brother was close to tears. Then he heard his mother's soft voice. "There, there, Will, we must do better than this." She brushed his tumbled hair from his eyes.

"But, Mama, I don't want to leave here. Do you?"

"N-no, I don't. All my friends are here." She hesitated. "But it means so very much to your father, we must not give way to our feelings. Glasgow and Nancy are young and look on this as a great adventure. We must learn to take it that way, too."

The Major overheard her, and his voice was gruff when he cleared his throat and asked, "Glasgow! Which side is starboard?"

"As you face the front of the ship, sir"—Glasgow turned and stood straight as a board—"larboard is on your left and starboard on your right!"

"Correct. Only a ship has no front," continued his father. "Facing the bow of the ship, the back is the stern. Only land-lubbers say 'front' and 'back.' But come, help me mend the harness." With a hand on the small boy's shoulder he moved toward the barn.

Soon the Major's commission as sailing master came through and he arranged to sell the farm and all the stock at Stony Point. After showing young Brady how to build a keelboat, at the end of April he traveled to Nashville—then on to Natchez, where he took boat for New Orleans. In July he assumed command of Gunboat No. 13.

Back at Stony Point, Glasgow stayed close to Merrill Brady building the keelboat, running errands for him to the farmhouse, fetching tools or lengths of rope. One day he watched young Brady carefully choose the trees for size. After he felled and trimmed them, he had the logs dragged to the new slide which went straight to the water's edge.

Brady was swinging away at a large V cut in a thick oak trunk, the ax slicing toward the heart of the tree, the ropes tied to pull it in the opposite direction when it fell. The tree swayed properly and Brady flung his ax aside, stepping back with pride. But the great oak snapped back violently and came crashing down toward Brady. He leaped to the right and back, tripping over Glasgow just behind him. Gaining his feet, he grabbed the boy—somersaulting and rolling with him to the bottom of a small gulley filled with ferns. The trunk splintered; the tree thundered down, its long branches crashing over Brady and Glasgow, just grazing them as they crouched in the hollow.

When the tree lay still, Brady pushed through the branches—pulling Glasgow after him. "Whew! That was close! You hurt?" Without waiting for an answer he said, "You're so little, I reckon the tree didn't touch you."

"I'm all right, Merrill." The boy tried to make his voice sound steady. Why was it people were always saying that he was small for his age?

"Lucky not to get killed," Brady growled, more relieved than he wanted to let on. "From here in you stay out of the woods when I'm chopping."

Glasgow's lips trembled, but he would not cry.

"Now look, friend," Brady said more kindly. "You go help

Will make the stobs, and I'll call you when I need you. I'll be taking off a few more branches before your mother calls us to dinner."

By early fall, with two men helping, Brady finished the boat, and Glasgow saw the double planks which reinforced the bottom so that no snags could rip it out. All around the upper edge was planking three feet high, to keep the children and animals from washing overboard. Half the deck was covered so that Mrs. Farragut could store her walnut table and its benches.

"Here, boys," she called. "Help me wrap these quilts around them. Then we can pile other things on top of them." Her hickory rocking chair went last. "I'll need that to rock the babies to sleep," she said.

A pen for the cow and other livestock was fenced in, and food for the animals and family had to be stored. Their water would come from the fresh rivers. Forward on each side of the boat were two oars in case of emergency, while directly astern was a large oar or setting pole for steering.

Now the Farragut family and crew of six were ready for the long voyage to New Orleans. As Merrill Brady shoved off with a long pole, neighbors and relatives called good-byes while the keelboat floated out on the river.

"Good-bye, good-bye!" Glasgow and Nancy shouted to the folks on the banks who waved handkerchiefs and aprons to the departing family. Glasgow stood in the bow, eyes straight ahead, hand on Skipper's shoulder, while Will made a great show of battening down everything. Glasgow knew his older brother could not bear to look back at his friends. And his mother, holding George Antoine, was staring back at Stony Point, crying.

Down at Campbell's Station they took on two rivermen,

Morgan and Tom Shaw, who were old-timers at steering a boat down the Mississippi. Though the great river shifted backward and forward, Tom Shaw knew all its twistings.

The Farraguts, Glasgow knew, would travel seventeen hundred miles and it would take them about seventy-five days, with Merrill Brady as Captain and Mrs. Farragut doing the cooking and mending for everyone.

Glasgow stayed topside all day, and in calm waters Brady let him stand at the helm; so the boy imagined himself master of a great ship on deep waters. But whenever Nancy helped her mother wash and mend clothes, he had to look after little George Antoine. He grumbled to Will, "Why do I always have to tend the baby?"

"Because he would fall overboard and drown, that's why," Will said practically—going right on sorting boxes and chests, as he was in charge of supplies. Just in time Glasgow rescued George Antoine from under a coil of rope. "See?" Will pointed to the spot where his brother crawled through with the baby. "You're small enough to wriggle after him when he gets into trouble."

Glasgow was glad when they reached the Tennessee River—the spot the Indians called the Boiling Pot, named for the wicked churnings of the river below the towering Chatanuga Mountain —and now Nancy had to tend George Antoine.

They made the hairpin turn around Moccasin Bend, and found not one white settlement in sight.

Sometimes Brady steered into shore; and then the children ran on the banks to stretch their legs, while the men gathered firewood and Brady shot wild turkeys and pigeons for the Farraguts' kettles. Will found a spring under a rock ringed with ferns. "Doesn't that taste good after the old river water?" he asked Glasgow as Nancy cupped her hands to hold the cool draught and lift it to her mouth.

"It is cold and fresh," said Mrs. Farragut, "so easy now; don't drown in it." But George Antoine almost did just that. He lay on his stomach and tried to lap up the water like Skipper.

Back on the boat again, Glasgow watched as they floated past Cherokee towns and Indian farms, seeing buffalo and deer come down to the river's edge to drink. When they moved north into the broad Ohio, the breeze stirred foamy whitecaps on the water as far as they could see; and the boys caught fish every day. Then the flatboat turned into the Mississippi, and Tom Shaw had to steer past the sand bars and islands that loomed up in the fog.

Treacherous twists in the river and a strong wind with the current made the boat leap and tug. "Slow her down!" bawled Tom Shaw, holding fast to the steering pole, and the two men sprang to hold it firm.

Then Morgan threw a long rope around a huge stump on the shore. "That should check her," he said, pulling the end tight. Brady helped him make it fast.

"Down the stream with the current is easy," Glasgow heard Morgan say, "but going back, Brady, ye'll be needin' twice the men ye have now. I understand the Major is giving ye the keelboat for bringing his family to New Orleans. Right handsome of him."

Farther on, Glasgow saw geese flying south in great wedges and, now and again, eagles circling overhead. But best of all were the many boats. There were great rafts and heavy flatboats, loaded with flour, tobacco, salt meat in barrels, bales of clothes, ironstuff —most of which was to be sold in New Orleans. One day he saw one of these drift to a settlement on the river bank where a man on the wharf blew a horn and the townfolk came running down to the landing to buy.

At other times he saw queer vessels like Noah's ark, with a house in the middle, and in the early evening he heard fiddling, singing, and dancing on these boats. Most of the people on river boats seemed jolly and friendly.

Long canoes glided past, paddled by trappers with heavy beards and faces burned as dark as any Indian's. They wore fringed deerskin clothes and coonskin caps, and their canoes were laden with bales of furs.

"Those trappers will be rich when they sell their furs in New Orleans," said Morgan, "if river pirates don't rob them before."

"And if they don't spend all their money down there before they come home," added Tom Shaw.

Near the end of their long journey the Farraguts saw the great cypress and live-oak trees, the latter draped with long gray beards of Spanish moss. The huge, ugly alligators lying close by the river's edge frightened Nancy, but she liked the white pelicans with the long yellow beaks and full pouches that swam and dived in the water. Sea gulls skimmed by gracefully, uttering harsh cries.

"Look"—Glasgow pointed ahead—"seems as if we're going to bump right into land."

"Does so," Tom Shaw agreed, "but this old river turns before we do that. It doubles back in the direction from which we came."

They had struck no snags and they had not seen any river pirates. Now roofs and spires appeared on the land and, on the river, clusters of masts lining the levee. Brady steered the boat safely on the wide curved sweep of the water front, and tied up for the night at the wharf above New Orleans. Then he went off in the skiff with Tom Shaw to let Major Farragut know his family had arrived.

Next morning they were all excited as Morgan brought the ship into port. There, waiting on the docks, stood Major Farragut with a tall old gentleman in naval uniform. The children climbed up the ladder and hurled themselves at their father, hugging and kissing him.

"How about this one?" asked Tom Shaw as he put George Antoine ashore. The baby slid down the planks into his father's arms.

"Do you remember me?" asked Major Farragut, tossing the baby into the air. Then he introduced the gentleman with him— Captain David Porter.

"I am glad you have come, Mrs. Farragut," chuckled Captain Porter. "We could not check your husband's taste for adventure."

"Adventure?" asked Mrs. Farragut.

"Yes. All alone, madam, your husband journeyed from New Orleans to Havana and back—in a pirogue!"

"Pirogue?" they all repeated.

"Yes, a sort of canoe made of two hollowed-out tree trunks joined together. He took it across the Gulf and back in mighty rough seas."

Mrs. Farragut shook her head, but smiled; and Glasgow beamed at his father, nearly bursting with pride.

"I will tell you all about it later," the Major said, laughing. "Now let's get into the carriage and go to our new home."

Their things were loaded into a horsedrawn cart. Merrill Brady climbed up next to the Negro driver, and the cart followed the carriage over the great wooden blocks that paved the streets.

4

Life in New Orleans

THE new one-and-a-half-story cottage with living quarters raised off the ground and a veranda around three sides looked like a plantation home. Thick batten blinds covered the long windows, and from the gardens came the sweet fragrance of the great white flowers on the tall magnolia trees outside. Nancy liked the vermilion blossoms of the pomegranate tree best, but Glasgow's favorite was the flat-leaved fig tree.

This strange new world brought many changes to the household, most important of which was the coming of Hercule and Toinette, whose master had set them free before he died. Toinette took over much of the hard work from Mrs. Farragut, including the shopping and marketing; and when Glasgow's mother objected, the sensible answer was, "Can Madame bargain in a foreign tongue?" With its ten thousand people of mixed races, Spanish and French were the languages spoken in the market places of New Orleans.

The Lafitte brothers had a blacksmith shop in the city where they sold the loot they pirated from ships in the rivers and the Gulf. The dirty streets of unpleasant odors, but rich with exotic merchandise from the ports of the world, were so different from the clean and simple wilderness of their Tennessee home at Stony Point.

Glasgow knew his mother felt Toinette competent to take over the marketing and other duties, and that she was happy to have the Negro woman to rely on; for she was expecting another baby. On November the twelfth Elizabeth was born. Now both Nancy and Mrs. Farragut had enough to do looking after a tiny baby and chubby George Antoine, too.

Hercule had complete charge of the boys. He took them through every alley and courtyard in the Vieu Carre, describing the great fire of 1788 that swept the city. The Farragut home was located in the new section above the moat (canal) dug around the great wall enclosing the town. But Glasgow liked it best when Hercule took them to the docks, where there were piles of bananas, sugar, indigo, sweet rare spices and herbs, tobacco, and coffee from the tropics. He watched powerful Negroes loading and unloading strange cargoes from all parts of the world, and studied all kinds of vessels.

One day they went to see a puppet show in the Place d'Armes entitled *The Deluge*. Glasgow and Hercule were so absorbed watching as Noah marched his animals two by two into his ark that they did not see Will and their dog, Skipper, wander off across the square to the levee.

"Maybe he's gone up the river," Glasgow suggested when they missed Will after the show. And they did find him there, waving good-bye to some rivermen in flatboats.

"They came from our Cumberland country back home," Will said wistfully, "and they know Merrill Brady's family, too."

But before long Will forgot his homesickness, for he received his commission in the United States Navy!

Glasgow knew that a boy could become a midshipman in the Navy if some higher officer recommended him, and when he got his commission he went aboard ship to learn to be a naval officer. After years of service he could be promoted to the next rank, that of lieutenant. Major Farragut, as sailing master, had sent in Will's name, and now at ten his older son was a midshipman! Glasgow was proud of his brother, who looked so handsome in his new uniform with its shiny gold buttons; but he wondered how *he* could get an appointment, since there was but one to a family to be had.

Shortly before, Major Farragut had bought a plantation on the Pascagoula River near Lake Pontchartrain, where he kept his gunboat at anchor. To navigate the lake he bought a yawl and, with Will gone, Glasgow spent much time with his father, who taught him how to hoist sails, furl them, coil the ropes, and on calm days take the helm.

One day when they were sailing on the lake, black clouds loomed up suddenly and the Major put the yawl about and headed for shore. The strong wind whipped the waves higher and higher. The tiny vessel dipped and rose to meet each wave, but they could make no headway. Salt water splashed into Glasgow's face as he clutched the side of the yawl and held on to his seat. He was sure the next wave would swallow them up, but soon they passed a gunboat.

"Come aboard until the blow is over," the Captain shouted.

The Major cupped his hands and called back, "I can ride it out, thank you, sir!"—and just then down came the rain, drenching them to the skin.

Finally the wind slackened, the waves quieted, and the Major was able to bring the yawl in to land. Already Glasgow had forgotten his fright and thought of it only as a grand adventure.

That spring of 1808 the children made many trips with their father to their plantation. Supplies had to be brought, and repairs had to be made on the house, the farm buildings, and the wharf. Nancy and George Antoine loved sailing almost as much as Glasgow, and all three soon were copper-colored as young Indians under the southern sun. Toinette scolded Nancy for becoming freckled and made her wear a straw bonnet and a veil wrapped around her head. But as soon as Toinette was out of sight, off they came!

Sometimes the Major and the children would be gone for days. If it rained, they slept wrapped deep in boat sails. If it was chilly, they dug holes in the sand and slept on the beach, covered with dry, warm sand. "Now is the time to harden them," the Major used to say as he gazed as his healthy, sun-browned children, "and to conquer any fears they may have." On Lake Pontchartrain, Glasgow—the future first Admiral—absorbed "the feel of the sea."

With the hot days upon them the family moved to their summer home, loving its large square rooms raised a story off the ground and resting on solid brick supports. On the ground floor was a large kitchen and workroom, and a veranda across the front of which rose narrow, short columns to the sloping roof above. Broad stairs led from the veranda to the yard, and from here to the wharf below was a long shaded avenue of moss-hung oak trees.

Occasionally the Major took the children in the pirogue up into the back country, and other times to the mouth of the river. There the fishermen cast their nets for shrimp; and Glasgow helped Nancy and George Antoine bait their lines for crabs, which Toinette made into gumbo (soup) next day.

But Glasgow liked best the long fishing trips on the yawl alone with his father, starting out at dark and sailing silently along in the night. Then the dawn would come up, lighting the sky, and the waters of Lake Pontchartrain would glow with its pale rose reflection.

Out for a sail on a morning late in June, they saw a small boat drifting close to the marsh grasses offshore. Pulling near, they made out the figure of a man, huddled over, clutching a fishing pole. "Ahoy there!" the Major hailed, and Glasgow thought it strange the man did not straighten up to answer. Drawing alongside, they found it was Captain David Porter, who seemed to have suffered a stroke.

When they got him to the plantation, Mrs. Farragut at once took over caring for him while the Major hurried off for a doctor. For days Captain Porter grew weaker and weaker, and Glasgow's mother wore herself out making him comfortable. Soon she fell ill with the dreaded yellow fever and had not the strength to throw it off. The old Captain passed away and Mrs. Farragut died shortly after, their funerals being held on the same day, June 24, 1808.

In the sad weeks that followed, Toinette had her hands full with the children. George Antoine often cried, asking when Mama would come. Nancy tried to make sailor dolls to amuse him, but she missed her mother terribly and often shut herself up in her room to cry. Will did not come home as often as before—and soon not at all. Glasgow knew how he felt—every time he came home there was something to remind him that their mother was gone.

During this time Glasgow learned to be quite independent, going away by himself to be alone with his grief. He talked with old sailors about ships and the sea, learning much about different vessels and sailing.

Then, because of poor health, Major Farragut gave up his position as sailing master and also the New Orleans home, moving the family out to the plantation.

Five days before Captain Porter had died, his son David had come to New Orleans as naval commander. He also took sick with the yellow fever. On his recovery, realizing the kindness of the Farraguts toward his sick father, in the fall of 1808 he went out to Pascagoula to express his thanks. Resplendent in his blue uniform and gold braid, he was a noble figure and Glasgow could not admire him enough.

The Major said, "This, Commander, is my second son, Glasgow. He may make a sailor himself someday." The boy stood taller, knowing his father thought he would make a good sailor.

After supper the two men smoked in the yard, while Glasgow sat on the cypress bench watching Nancy and George Antoine chasing fireflies.

"Major, I don't know what you will think of this idea," Commander Porter was saying, "but it's been in my mind and heart for some time. Your fine wife took care of my father as a daughter would. Let me take care of Glasgow. If he is living in my household I can get him commissioned in the Navy, as you did for Will. My infant son is so frail I fear he will never grow to stand the rigors of the service."

The Major nodded, slowly, wearily, as Porter continued. "Your own ill health imposes an added burden on you in raising the children. Toinette is fine for little George Antoine and baby Elizabeth. But what about Nancy? Let her come with Glasgow. Mrs. Porter can give her all the fancy training a young lady should have."

Major Farragut stared at his son. "Glasgow, how would you

like to live with Commander Porter? When you reach midshipman's years, you can enter the Navy."

Glasgow could scarcely hide his excitement. "Oh, sir, there's nothing I'd rather be than a midshipman in the Navy!" he cried.

"Better think about it," the Commander suggested. "Sleep on it. You'll come to live with my family at first, but life at sea is long and lonely. You never are your own boss, you know."

That night while his father and the Commander still talked, Glasgow lay tossing under his mosquito net, unable to sleep. It would mean leaving this home; but with his mother gone, he felt restless. He thought of Will. If his brother could stand living away from home, so could he. Besides, this was his chance for a commission! He fell asleep dreaming of great adventures and sea battles.

Late that fall Glasgow and Nancy went to live with the Porters, Nancy to stay with them as long as the Commander was stationed in New Orleans. Mrs. Porter tried to make them feel at home; but it was not easy, for they felt strange in this beautiful house. At the dinner table, set with crystal and silver, Glasgow seemed lost in a tall carved chair, and he saw that Nancy, sitting across from him, appeared unhappy. Both missed their customary tableful of noisy, happy children back at Pascagoula.

At the end of the meal Commander Porter rose. "Children, I have a surprise for you," he said, and left the room. Returning in a few moments, he held out his hands gently; and there, wrapped in a snowy blanket, lay a tiny baby. It waved its fists in the air, and Nancy came running around to see. Why, the baby was scarcely as large as one of her dolls!

"This is my son, William Porter," said the Commander proudly. "He was so small when he was born that for months he slept in a cigar box. Too tiny to be dressed, he had to be wrapped in cotton wool." The baby cooed and kicked its tiny heels, and suddenly the children felt at home. Why, Commander Porter was just like their father, who loved to give them pleasant surprises!

Glasgow was sent to school in New Orleans; but there were still sailing trips with his father on the lake, and sometimes Commander Porter took the boy with him on short cruises down the river.

In April of 1809 the Commander was called to Washington on official business, and Glasgow was to sail with him on the bomb brig *Vesuvius.* Nancy was to live with Commander Porter's sister, whose husband was a doctor at the naval station.

On the day of the departure Major Farragut said good-bye to his son; gave him a book; then stood on shore, waving until he could no longer see the *Vesuvius.* Glasgow, with tears in his eyes, looked at his father's gift. On the flyleaf he saw his father's name, his mother's name, his own and all the children's names. It was their family Bible, with dates of birth and death.

Glasgow would, in time, have to enter the date of the Major's death in it, for he never again saw his father alive.

5

A Midshipman at Nine

COMMANDER PORTER spent some time in Washington, trying to collect his reward for capturing a pirate ship, while Glasgow enjoyed the days watching the vessels on the Potomac and talking to sailors. Then the family moved to Chester, Pennsylvania.

Months passed, and Christmas came. A tall fir tree stood in the corner of the drawing room, and it was a thing of wonder to Glasgow; for, living in the South, he had never seen a Christmas tree. He was anxious to get this one finished, and helped twist colored paper into various shapes while Mrs. Porter threaded popcorn. Every so often he jumped up to look through the window at the snow falling outside; for he had seldom seen snow, and never in such quantity.

"A fine Christmas, my boy," Commander Porter smiled. "Tomorrow we shall get the sleigh out for church."

Glasgow wished it were tomorrow now, for the Commander had promised him a fine present and a gift. He didn't quite understand this distinction, for Commander Porter had added he was sure to like the first and might like the second.

"When will we light the candles?" Glasgow asked as they finished trimming the tree, for he wanted to see the bright flames glitter.

"As soon as it is dark; for just a little while, though," Mrs. Porter promised. "We'll light them again in the morning, when the presents are distributed. Can you guess what you are receiving?"

"N-no, I can't guess," he answered as they arranged the packages around the tree.

Christmas morning Glasgow was up early, but, first, prayers had to be said and then all the servants received their presents. Finally came the big surprise. Right on top of Glasgow's pile of gifts lay a thin Navy packet addressed to Mr. David Glasgow Farragut, in care of Commander David Porter, U.S.N.

"Your midshipman's warrant from the Navy Department in Washington," said Commander Porter, smiling.

Glasgow waved the papers in the air, beside himself with joy. Abruptly he halted, drew to attention in front of the Commander, and gave him a smart salute—his first in the Navy.

"What a wonderful Christmas present, sir!" he cried.

"Mr. Secretary made good his promise, didn't he?" asked Commander Porter. "A midshipman by the time you were ten. Let's see, this was issued December 17, 1810, when you were exactly nine years, five months, and twelve days old!"

"Right, sir, and many thanks to you." The boy felt the Commander's hand on his shoulder and, glancing up into his kind, solemn face grew serious at once.

"My boy, you have your present. We are proud of you, and we know you will make us still prouder as you continue in the service. I want you now to have your gift, and I hope it will please you as much. I give you my name, David. It will please Mrs. Porter and me if you will bear it, as a representative of our household. In your excitement you did not scan the warrant closely. Look again."

Glasgow read the document carefully, and there it was: "David Glasgow Farragut"—not "James Glasgow Farragut." It made no difference; no one ever called him James. Besides, David was a fine name. Little David had slain Goliath. Why, Commander Porter's gift was wonderful! It made him all warm inside, and he could only say in a low voice, "Thank you, sir. I hope I may honor the name."

Shortly after, Commander Porter brought a small package home and handed it to David Glasgow. Opening it, the new midshipman gasped with delight. In a leather case lay a beautiful gold watch, inscribed "From D.P. to D.G.F., U.S.N., 1810."

"Not many nine-year-old boys own a gold watch," thought David.

After the New Year, Commander Porter received another post —that of acting Captain of the frigate *Essex*. In midsummer another long, official envelope came for Midshipman David Glasgow Farragut. It read: "*You are hereby ordered to repair on board the United States Frigate Essex, now lying at Norfolk, Virginia, where you will enter upon the duties of a midshipman.*" David's first orders!

One hot day in August, Commander Porter and Midshipman Farragut climbed up on a stagecoach going south, the latter's friends gathering round to say good-bye. The young fellows looked on with envy; but the grownups smiled at the sight of uniformed ten-year-old David, small for his age, the high cocked hat he wore seeming top-heavy above his solemn little oval face.

The driver cracked his whip over the horses, and everyone cheered. The coach rumbled away in a cloud of dust. After hours of driving in the heat and dust, David wished he had taken Mrs. Porter's advice. "Wear your civilian clothes," she had said. "Then your uniform will be fresh in your portmanteau."

Now, seated behind the driver, David sweated, and soon his white waistcoat, knee breeches, and stockings were covered with a thick gray coating of dust. He jounced about, his legs too short to reach the footrest; but he sat erect, his hazel eyes fixed straight ahead. He had to hold hard to keep his seat; and as they rode on, the roads became worse. Once a wheel caught in a deep rut, pulling the lead horse down and toppling the coach.

David, in his once splendid uniform, was flung into a shallow brook, where the water and mud completed the havoc that perspiration and dust had begun. Fortunately no one was hurt, and everybody set to work righting the coach. Midshipman Farragut, more injured in pride than in body, dripping and muddy, helped to set the coach on the road and was glad a short time later when part of the journey from Baltimore to Norfolk was made by sailing packet. Sailing proved better than the bone-shaking, dusty ride on the stagecoach.

He found Norfolk a different seaport from New Orleans; for during the Revolution a British admiral had burned most of the town, so the houses were all tidy new brick buildings. Many ships lay idle along the wharves. Commander Porter explained that Norfolk had suffered from the Embargo Act, which, aimed against both France and England, had boomeranged on American commerce.

"We can't stand interference with our commerce much longer,

or there will have to be war," said Porter. "Perhaps the sooner the better!" They were walking through a gateway at the navy yard and, as they came onto the wharf in the Elizabeth River, the Commander continued, "There lies our ship, my boy," indicating the *Essex*, at anchor.

"Oh!" David cried out. "She's beautiful, sir!" He knew that she was a frigate and, though small, had fought against the pirates at Tripoli.

Commander Porter signaled, and soon a small boat put out from the frigate and picked David up. Aboard the frigate, he saluted Lieutenant Downes and delivered a note which ordered Midshipman Farragut to commute Commander Porter to and from the ship each day. The Lieutenant turned to a midshipman standing by. "Mr. Fittimary, this is Mr. Farragut. Show him to his quarters and see that his things are brought below."

David saluted, turned on his heel, and followed the older boy. Mr. Fittimary took David down the hatch to the steerage, pointed out his hammock and a locker for his clothes as a seaman dropped David's canvas bag beside him.

"Mr. Farragut," said Mr. Fittimary, "in New Orleans I knew your brother well. I'd like to call you David, and you may call me Merry."

Later David was especially glad he had Merry for a friend; for when the twelve midshipmen (or reefers) aboard came to meet the "new boy," he saw that they were all seventeen or eighteen years old and very much bigger than he. At ten, David Glasgow Farragut was the youngest midshipman ever to report for duty in the American Navy, and he suspected he would have a rugged time with the other "reefers."

That night after lights out David struggled with his hammock, suspended from hooks attached to the beams overhead. Looking over to where Merry was, he heard him whisper, "Just relax, fellow. You won't fall out."

For three long months the *Essex* lay at anchor being refitted, but Commander Porter used the days to explain his duties to David. "There is a time and a place for everything aboard ship. What you do now will show what kind of officer you will make later on. Every officer must know where everything is, how it is used, and how everything should be done."

"Yes, sir," David said smartly, his dark brown head raised high.

"Don't say 'Yes, sir' any more to an order," Porter suggested. "In our Navy it is a willing 'Aye, aye, sir.' "

"Aye, aye, sir," repeated David, his swarthy face rigidly at attention; his small body erect, at command.

Porter added, "On board ship you will be treated like every other midshipman; no favors granted. You must learn discipline in the Navy as soon as possible."

"Aye, aye, sir," David answered tersely.

So the ship became David's school. He found he did not have to worry about being seasick, for the rough rides on Lake Pontchartrain with his father had made him all but immune to that. He studied over and over all the parts of a ship: the guns called carronades, the square-rigged masts, and the maze of ropes—stays, shrouds, sheets, halyards—soon he had memorized them all.

He found what Captain Porter meant by discipline. Aboard a ship an officer's orders had to be obeyed promptly, with no complaints, no whining about injustice or cruelty. Life at sea would be hard, as Captain Porter had warned; but every man doing his duty meant the safety of all and of the ship.

The thing David hated most were the jokes of the other reefers. They sent him to look for five bells and left-handed rope stretchers; worst of all, they teased him about his size and age. Knowing he was quick on his feet, lean and strong as a wire, he wished he could settle it with one good fight. "One at a time I could lick them," he thought, balling his fists.

One day David was waiting at the wharf at Norfolk to take Commander Porter back to the *Essex*, and some dock loafers strolled over to watch the boat and crew. One of them pointed at David, sneering, "Funny, ain't it? Grown men taking orders from a fancy-dressed tyke like that!"

"I'd as soon take orders from me own young'un I whup once a week for caution's sake," laughed another.

David saw that his men were restless under the gibes, shifting about in their places as if to say, "What should we do?" His face felt hot as he grew angrier, and he saw Sam Riley, the bowman, grip his boat hook tighter.

Then the first dock walloper grabbed up an old pail and, leaning over the wharf, dipped it in the water and filled it. With a quick movement he dumped the water on top of Mr. Farragut's head, cackling, "That oughter help you to grow some."

David spluttered and reached for his dirk, but in a flash Sam Riley's boat hook caught the man by the pocket of his trousers. The other sailors joyfully leaped onto the wharf, with David sprinting along into the melee of fists, oars, and hooks. He slashed at a threatening blow; but almost immediately the crew chased the gang all the way into the Market Square, where the Norfolk police caught and arrested them all—wharf loungers, sailors, and Mr. David Farragut! Midshipman Farragut's name appeared on the police record: "Bound over to keep the peace. Bonds furnished."

Back on deck, David was chastened by Commander Porter, who had a strange quirk in his mouth as he delivered the stern lecture. "Of all things, to start your career in the Navy by aiding in a riot! What sort of discipline is that, Mr. Farragut?" David's ears burned from the scolding as he hurried down to his place in the steerage.

In his cabin, later, Commander Porter remarked with a chuckle to Lieutenant Downes, "My boy Farragut is three pounds of uniform and seventy pounds of fight. His men will follow him anywhere."

At the same moment, down below, an older reefer was saying, "Lor', I wish I'd seen it!"

From then on there was no more teasing David about his age or his size.

6

First Sea Fight

COMMANDER PORTER believed war with Great Britain might come any day, and cruised the *Essex* along the coast to protect American commerce against foreign interference. After final repairs on the ship were finished, the *Essex* sailed out of sight of land. Now there were drills at sea and target practice. A barrel was tossed overboard, the ports were thrown open, and the carronades were trained on the target. Like a trumpet came the order "Open Fire!" The carronades barked their loud thunder, and David thought he would never be able to hear again.

Then there were fire drills. Every man had to be ready with cutlass and blankets when the alarm sounded, for the crew never knew whether it was a real emergency or only a drill. Sometimes Commander Porter would start a bit of smoke in the main hold to make the practice realistic.

When off duty, David Glasgow liked to climb to the top of the mast and, glancing down, watch the crew crawling around like toy men far below. Once when the Commander asked, "Where's Mr. Farragut?" the answer came, "Aloft in the mast, sir, for fresh air." And William Kingsbury, boatswain's mate, hurried to explain, "But he's sure of foot as a cat, sir." So David was allowed to stay up. Yet when Kingsbury blew his silver pipe calling all hands, David was the first on deck.

By December the crew of the *Essex* was drilling so efficiently it was the best in the squadron. And now came orders to sail for Newport, Rhode Island. The entrance to the harbor was narrow, and on Christmas Eve their ship anchored off the bluffs to wait for favorable winds and tide to sail through.

That bitter cold night the midshipmen huddled below in the steerage with no stoves to keep them warm. Sam Riley got his fiddle out. The boys tried to do a sailor's hornpipe for exercise and warmth, but even poor Sam's fingers were stiff with cold; and though the Commander sent down red-hot cannon balls to drop into a tub of sand, it grew colder and colder. Finally the midshipmen climbed into their hammocks fully dressed, wrapped their blankets around them, and placed their pea jackets on top to keep from freezing.

All through the night the wind cut through the ship. By morning it was a shrieking gale, driving snow and sleet before it. The *Essex* pitched and rolled like a wild beast trying to break loose. Toward morning the crew was awakened by Mate Kingsbury's piping all hands. Spars, rigging, the bulwarks—everything was coated with ice. David saw the boys holding hard to anything and everything to keep from being washed overboard. He, too, clung for dear life as he inched his way along the deck.

Commander Porter and Lieutenant Downes took turns on the lookout for only a few minutes at a time, clinging to the hammock netting to keep afoot. The huge waves roared and hissed as they struck and broke over the rails, and icy brine drenched every man on deck. Suddenly David heard the sound of a dragging anchor. A second one was let go, but it didn't hold. Two more were dropped and still the ship drifted. David peered up at the icebound spars and rigging, topsails which could not be lowered to relieve the pressure, and then he heard a splintering crash. The main cord mizzen topgallant masts had blown away. Next a heavy shock that tumbled him off his feet told him that the ship had grounded.

"If we beat over this bank we're resting on," shouted Mate Kingsbury, "the whole of the masts may have to go. Stand by!"

Down below, axes in hand, the men stood ready to cut down the masts if the moment came, for they knew the danger of the ship's being hurled against the icy cliffs. Just when they thought all was lost, the wind slackened. The heavy seas subsided and, instead of pounding to pieces on the sand bar, the *Essex* floated off into deep water.

For weeks after this experience, anchored in the inner harbor at Newport while the ship was reconditioned, the midshipmen studied their textbooks with Mr. Adams, the chaplain. The boys were catching up in their journals, for every midshipman had to keep his log up to date. If, when inspection came, it was not written up, they would be punished; so their goose quills moved faster then a duck's tail.

In the spring the *Essex*, with Rodgers' squadron, was ordered to New York, and David found the next weeks dull. But on the eighteenth day of June he bounded down the hatch to shout, "It's happened! War's declared!"

"Joker, joker," the midshipmen shrugged.

"No, listen!" Sure enough, there was the call for all hands on the main deck.

When every man was present, Commander Porter read aloud the Declaration of War of 1812 against Great Britain. Men in the American Navy knew this war must be fought for two vital reasons involving freedom. In search for British seamen who had deserted from their fleet, English captains often "impressed" men from American merchant ships. Moreover, they claimed that any American trading ship that put into a port controlled by Napoleon could be seized by the British.

Thus was adopted the motto which Commander Porter announced: "FOR FREE TRADE AND SAILORS' RIGHTS!"

David joined in the hearty cheering.

Because the American Navy was small, the ships went out in squadrons to meet the enemy; and when Rodgers' squadron left New York, the Essex had to remain behind two weeks to be refitted with a new foremast. Then on July the second, Porter received his promotion to Captain and orders to sail in search of the Thetis, a British frigate.

All hands were eager to get to sea, but two days later was the Fourth of July, a national holiday, and special salutes were given at sunrise, noon, and sunset. The men enjoyed extra rations of grog and duff (plum pudding).

For David, July the fifth was much more important. Eleven years old, he walked with a manlier stride and carried his head higher. "Now I'm a regular old-timer in the Navy," he thought as once more he admired the engraving on his watch.

For six days the Essex cruised south, but the Thetis was not in sight. On July the eleventh Porter caught up with a convoy of seven transports taking one thousand British soldiers to Quebec.

Captain Porter ordered only enough men on deck to work the ship, while the rest lay flattened out close to the bulwarks. David hid behind a barrel. Flying a British flag, as many American merchant and frigate captains did to deceive the British cruisers, the *Essex* drew silently ahead into the fleet, and Porter called to a vessel to surrender.

"Who are you?" challenged the master, frantically trying to signal his escort, the *Minerva*.

The *Essex's* ports were thrown open and the enemy ship's master found himself facing powerful guns. "You are a prize of war. Give no alarm and follow as you value your ship!" ordered Captain Porter. The *Essex* withdrew with her prize, a brig with one hundred and ninety-seven British soldiers aboard.

"Sir," David asked, "will we engage their escort frigate, *Minerva*, with her thirty-two guns?"

"We will," Captain Porter said decisively. At dawn the decks were cleared for action; sail after sail was unfurled in man-of-war style, while the Stars and Stripes were run up the main and mizzen masts as the Union Jack came down.

The *Essex* held to the edge of the convoy, expecting to draw fire when within gunshot; but, instead, the *Minerva* tacked ship and fled among the convoy.

"Blast her, she's leaving us behind, Captain!" cried the quartermaster.

"Yes, she won't risk her convoy," said Captain Porter, smiling. "Doesn't know we have one of her chicks."

David saw their prisoners disarmed and paroled—released on their word of honor not to fight against the United States again during this war. Captain Porter then permitted the brig to go to Halifax under a ransom bond.

On August the thirteenth the *Essex*, sailing north, spied a British ship and, disguised as a merchantman, acted as though she were trying to escape the enemy. Falling into the trap, the English vessel closed in and fired on the *Essex* but did no damage. Porter ordered the American flag run up, and his guns readied in the open ports.

"Fire!" he commanded. The fuses in the touchholes were lighted from slow matches and, after a split second of sizzling, the guns roared, bucking back with the recoil. As the *Essex* battered away at the enemy's frame and rigging, David thrilled to his first smell of battle powder.

In eight minutes the enemy surrendered, and Captain Porter sent Lieutenant Finch aboard her to take possession. He found seven feet of water in her hold, and three men wounded. The injured were cared for and the leak repaired. Then David and Fittimary watched the crew of the new prize board the *Essex*. "Whew!" said Merry, shaking his head. "With the prisoners already aboard, this makes close to five hundred we have."

"Two Britishers to every American!" David murmured thoughtfully. The danger of being outnumbered stayed with him, and he resolved to be on the alert.

One night, just before dawn, he came awake suddenly, sensing something amiss. But what was it? He pretended to be asleep, not moving a muscle; but he could not hear a thing. His heart pounded loudly as he held his breath.

There was the sound of a slight movement as a great hulking form bent over his hammock. David shut his eyes, but not before he had recognized the coxswain of the English Captain's gig. The man held a huge pistol in his uplifted hand, and the boy wondered if it was going to crash down on his head. He scarcely breathed and was thankful when the man turned away to cross the steerage and ascend the ladder. Waiting until he disappeared, David crept out of his hammock.

Quietly, in bare feet, he ran through the wardroom and up to the Captain's cabin. "Wake up, sir!" he cried. "Wake up! The prisoners are loose!"

Captain Porter sprang from his cot, hurried into his clothes, and buckled on his cutlass while David told his story. Snatching his pistol, he rushed onto the berth deck, his midshipman fast at his heels.

"Fire! Fire!" the Captain roared. He counted on his men, so well trained in fire drills that at the alarm every one of them would spring up and seize a cutlass and blanket and be ready at his station without lost motion. And so it happened. The mutineering prisoners, seeing armed men on every side and thinking it might be a real fire, became confused. They were subdued without a fight, and the coxswain, their ringleader, was put in irons. They had plotted to seize the Essex, then recapture their ship, the Alert, and sail victorious to Halifax.

After that no one cared for sleep and, as the cooks went to prepare breakfast, David descended to the steerage into a great surprise welcome.

"Here comes Mr. Farragut. Let's give three cheers for Mr. Farragut!" yelled Midshipman William Feltus, and his fellow officers shouted their acclamations.

David grinned, feeling his neck getting hotter and hotter.

"If you hadn't got us out of bed this night, David," bellowed Merry, "we might all be bound for Halifax this very minute. But, instead, Captain Porter has kindly released all the prisoners, given them back the Alert, and sent them on parole to Halifax."

"That's not the way they planned it." David shook his head. "But perhaps it's just as well for those poor press-gang devils."

Later, after breakfast, with the cheers of the young officers still echoing in his ears, he received even higher praise from Captain Porter. "David, my boy, I said I'd be proud of you, and I am. No man in the same dangerous situation could have acted with more courage, alacrity, and intelligence."

Around the Horn to Strange Sights

I N taking the *Alert*, the *Essex* made the first capture of a British
man-of-war in the War of 1812; and all the men were in high
spirits, for seamen and officers would share in the prize money.
Now, lying at Chester, Pennsylvania, Captain Porter received
orders on October 6, 1812, to prepare the *Essex* for a long cruise.

David saw the men load lime juice, fresh fruits, vegetables,
salt, live goats, chickens, pigs, beef, pork and beans, bread and
drinking water. Where were they bound for now, he wondered,
for all these supplies would last them months! When he saw the
clothing for all seasons coming aboard, he knew the cruise might
last a year or longer. Finally, round shot, grape canister, wads,
and gun powder for the ammunition room were stowed in the
holds.

As always, everything must be shipshape on the *Essex*; for

though she was the smallest frigate in the squadron, she was the "smartest ship in the Navy." That's what David had heard Rodgers tell Captain Porter in New York. Now the *Essex* was to cross the Atlantic to meet the *Constitution* and the *Hornet* at the Cape Verde Islands, and from there the three ships were to destroy the British commerce in the South Atlantic.

The *Essex* had hopes of captures on her way across the ocean, but every time she overtook a vessel it turned out to be a Portuguese ship. Once, in the mid-Atlantic, a great gale struck her, flooding her decks, ruining many of the provisions, and soaking bedding and clothing. Still on they sailed while the boys continued to learn mathematics and navigation, and drilled, drilled, drilled!

After a fast voyage of twenty-nine days at sea, covering thirty-five hundred miles of water, the *Essex* arrived at the Cape Verde Islands, looking for but not meeting Captain Bainbridge and his waiting ship. The Portuguese were friendly, though, helping with fresh provisions and water; and now the *Essex* sailed on for Brazil, where Bainbridge had proceeded.

Late in November, David heard the older men whisper about "crossing the line" and knew it meant a rough initiation for anyone who had never crossed the equator before.

On the day of crossing, David's old friend Kingsbury appeared over the side dressed as Father Neptune, master of ceremony. Beside him stood a fat seaman posing as Neptune's wife, Amphitrite. These two proceeded to conduct the initiations, while officers and crew looked on as one victim after another was put through the ordeal.

"Mis-s-ter-r Farragut," roared Neptune.

David grinned as he stepped forward.

"Lay aloft on the spar, sir!"

The boy climbed up onto the spar and sat there, clinging

tightly to his clumsy perch; for beneath him was a tub of salt water.

Neptune and Amphitrite daubed his face with soap, grease, and tar; then, with an elaborate show of care, they shaved off this "lather" with a huge wooden razor. Unexpectedly they toppled David off into the tub of water, while the onlookers roared and cheered and laughed at the great splash he made. Wanting to show the others he could take it, the boy climbed out, dripping but smiling, and went off to find dry clothes and to scour his face.

A few days later David decided he must show further proof that he was a regular he-man. He knew that most seafaring men chewed tobacco, and anyone who didn't "chaw" might be called a sissy. So this day he was manfully struggling with a cut of tobacco in his mouth when he spied Captain Porter approaching. David stopped chewing and clamped his jaws tight, hoping the Captain would not notice his bulging cheeks. But unfortunately a sticky brown trickle began to ooze from the corner of his mouth.

"Mr. Farragut, come here," the Captain ordered. David moved forward and came to attention. "Swallow!" was the stern command.

David had to gulp several times to force the quid down, but he obeyed the painful order. Captain Porter strode away. Never was David sicker, and from that day never did he chew tobacco again. The very smell of it would bring back the horrible sensation he had in his stomach after he had swallowed the quid.

After crossing the equator a sail was discovered to windward. "Sail ho!" the lookout cried, anxious for a fight and prize. The *Essex* promptly ran up the British flag signal captured from the *Alert*, but the strange ship would not be lured within range of its guns. They chased her for hours; and as they came closer,

David could see it was a brig of war with English colors. The *Essex* kept up her chase, and Captain Porter, hoping to take her without gunfire, navigated his vessel alongside her.

"Ship ahoy!" he shouted. "Stand to surrender!" Abruptly the brig put her wheel over as if to ram the *Essex*.

"Sir," David cried, "she's trying to run under our stern and escape."

Captain Porter nodded and brought the *Essex* around suddenly, the change of course cutting off the brig's escape. He raised his hand. The men in the tops fired a volley, and the brig struck her colors.

The prize this time was the British *Nocton*, bound for Falmouth, with thirty-one men aboard, armed with ten guns and fifty-five thousand dollars in money! Captain Porter took the money and the prisoners in hand; then he gave Lieutenant Finch a small crew from the *Essex*, ordering him to make with them for the nearest American port.

Three days later, on the island of Fernando de Noronha, Captain Porter read a letter from Bainbridge with instructions to meet him off Cape Frio, northward of Rio de Janeiro. Cruising off that port during Christmas week, the *Essex* captured one small prize but still had not seen her sister ships. Sailing northward up the coast, Porter learned from passing Portuguese vessels that both the *Hornet* and the *Constitution* had been forced by the enemy to put out to sea.

Now the Captain was free to choose his own course, and Daivd knew that the men would not want to start for home with only two small prizes. Why, in three months at sea, scarcely a gun had been fired! He was glad when the Captain called in the men to present his plan.

Captain Porter informed them they had bread for only three months at half allowance, and it was too dangerous to put in at any port for provisions. Also it was sure death or capture to try to return to the United States, for the waters swarmed with enemy ships. "So, men," Captain Porter proposed, "I want the *Essex* to double Cape Horn! We'll find supplies at a port in Chile, and cruise the Pacific alone."

"Captain," Lieutenant Downes offered, "one thing is in our favor, sir. The enemy will not suspect our presence there now." David's hazel eyes lighted with pleasure at the thought of dangerous surprise attacks on unsuspecting Britishers, and saw that the men felt much the same as he did about it.

"Yes, but we must move quickly," continued Porter. "Take him unawares in the Pacific and cripple British commerce before England can send a fleet strong enough to drive us out. However, if they get scent of this—"

They all knew what that meant as they shouted, "Aye, aye, sir! It is a chance we should take. Any man who betrays us will pay the penalty." The crew was eager to begin its twenty-five-hundred-mile voyage around the Horn.

But Boatswain's Mate Kingsbury shook his head. "January ain't the time of year for doubling the Horn, especially the westward passage."

"His voice is mournful as an old owl's," David thought. Aloud he asked, "Don't you think we can make it?"

Pointing to Captain Porter on the quarter-deck, Kingsbury's gloomy answer was, "With *him*, and the Lord's help, we will."

The weather remained mild until the middle of February, and the midshipmen taunted Kingsbury. "Where are your mighty horrors of the Horn?" David's swarthy jaw set as he saw Kingsbury freeze.

"We've not rounded her yet, and she's not to be made light of; for she's got endless tricks up her sleeve a human can't suspect until he knows her."

The others laughed, but David didn't. He knew Kingsbury was an old sailor who had been around the Horn before. By noon that very day the first terrible storm came up, and the crew hurried to reef the sails to ride it out.

"Hard times ahead," prophesied Kingsbury. "This is only a taste of what's to be." David heard the ripping of canvas as it tore away in the wind.

For two weeks the Essex battled icebergs, sudden gales, driving rain, and swirling snow, while the steady northerly winds drove her far south of her intended course. The men pulled on layer after layer of clothing to keep warm. The ship pitched and rolled, and again and again David and the others were sent to furl or unfurl canvas heavy with rain and snow.

One day as Captain Porter made a hurried entry in the ship's log, he ordered, "Mr. Farragut, stand by."

"Aye, aye, sir!" David's slender body was rigid at attention although he was tired and hungry. Rations were low; the crew was on half allowance of food and water, for much of the dried-food provisions were full of weevils.

"We will have to pull our belts in another notch, David." Porter turned to the boy. "We're not through yet and, please God, we'll make it if we all keep faith and stout courage."

Captain Porter stood up. David had just handed him his hat when a huge wave broke over the ship's side, causing her to heel violently, and sent David sprawling. He got up painfully to follow his capatin to the gun deck, where they saw the ports were stove in from bow to quarter and that the sea water was heaving in.

"The keelboat's gone on the quarter-deck, sir," reported Bowman Riley. "The weather quarter boat held at the wheel, but the extra spars washed overboard."

"Kingsbury!" shouted the Captain. "Get the crew to work below immediately!"

David followed Kingsbury, and halfway down the ladder they heard the boatswain shouting, "Our starboard is stove in and shipping the whole bloody ocean!"

Torrents of water poured into the hatchway and, as the small vessel lurched, David saw fear in the sailors' faces. One man fell to his knees, praying, and several others were too paralyzed with terror to do anything.

While the water swirled about his knees and the ship reeled with each surge of the sea, Kingsbury roared, "Blast your eyes! Up with you! Put your best foot forward. There's still the port side of the Essex left."

After patching the damage and pumping out the water that threatened to sink their ship, the crew followed Kingsbury to the gun deck. All hands fell to, cleared away the wreckage, and secured the small boats. Then they put their stout frigate before the wind; and the Essex lifted her head once more to ride the seas proudly, the first American man-of-war to double Cape Horn. A week later she was at anchor, safe in the broad, calm waters of the Pacific off the island of Mocha.

Yellow sands and, beyond, the green of forests on the mountains. "What a welcome relief!" thought David—and a chance to take on needed food and fresh water. Armed with muskets, hunting parties pushed off from the ship in the small boats. David felt the beach rocking under him as he started to walk, but he soon found his land legs. He helped to dig pits in the sand, set up forked sticks on which to smoke meat. The hunters came back with droves of hogs, even a herd of wild horses, and by sundown the boats carried back to the Essex fresh pork to be eaten immediately and smoked pork and salted horse meat for the weeks ahead.

Now Captain Porter put in for Valparaiso on the coast of Chile. In Spanish the name of this seaport meant "Valley of Paradise," and after being at sea for nearly four months it looked like paradise to the crew.

Lieutenant Downes was sent ashore to see if the people would welcome them, and returned with good news. Chile had revolted against Spain and would be happy to sell the Americans all the supplies they wanted. The *Essex* was the first American frigate to drop anchor in their harbor.

David had learned Spanish from his father, so Porter asked him to interpret in the official exchange of courtesies between the Captain and Governor.

Out came long-unused cocked hats and gold-laced coats as two magnificent balls were given on shore for the Americans. A dinner and dance on the *Essex* followed for the Chilean officials and their ladies. The deck was gay with flags, while mess attendants in spotless white trousers waited on table in the Captain's cabin. There were toasts to the Republic of the United States, then to the Republic of Chile, which everybody applauded. David knew that many did not know what they were clapping for.

After dinner formal square dances were held on the spar deck in the open air, with the ship's band fiddling and blaring its best on the poop. Older midshipmen pranced about, but David, being only a boy, had to be satisfied just to look on.

There was much work yet to do, for the *Essex* must be fitted out for her campaign in the Pacific. Casks had to be filled with fresh water, rolled down to the beach; then hoisted into the boats, rowed back to the frigate, and stowed in the hold. Fresh supplies of wood for the galley stove had to be cut and stored. Fresh vegetables and fruits, more salt beef and salt pork, too, were brought aboard.

In the privacy of his cabin Captain Porter told David some

news. "My boy, it's pleasant here and the men need the rest; but we have important work to do. Peru is sending out privateers to prey on our American whalers."

"You mean on our men from New Bedford and Nantucket?"

"Yes. We must get to sea quickly to protect these whalers as well as capture those flying the red ensign of England."

By the last of March all was ready and the supplies paid for with the prize money from the capture of the *Nocton*. Once more the *Essex* headed for the open sea.

Sailing northward up the coast, she made several small seizures —one of which was the *Barclay*, an American whaler that they recaptured from Peru. Then, as the Galápagos Islands, lying west of the coast of Ecuador, were a favorite gathering place for whalers, Porter set his course for them.

After anchoring in the islands, David accompanied the Captain ashore. "We are going to the post office," he smiled. This proved to be a box nailed to a tree near the landing. In it the whalers left newspapers and letters for each other, as well as notes telling of their arrivals and departures. These notes were what Porter wanted, for from them he learned where all the English whaling ships were.

For several weeks the *Essex* was based on the Galápagos, and David knew he would always remember those days on the Enchanted Islands as some of the happiest of his life. Often he and the boys went ashore, where flocks of pigeons swarmed about— many becoming potpie in the ship's galley. The midshipmen discovered a plentiful supply of very large and delicious prickly pears.

Once while standing watch, far over the horizon David saw something rare—the violent eruption of a volcano on the neighboring island of Narboro. He thought it looked as if the world were blowing up in a mass of flame and black smoke.

Daily the sailors were allowed ashore for amusement and exercise and, finding huge turtles, some weighing over three hundred pounds, they tried riding them. David climbed upon one, the other reefers teasing, and as it lurched from side to side he called out, "It's hard to stay aboard this rough-riding vessel."

Another day they ran their boats onto the beach at Devil's Rock, where they found seals making for the water. Someone called, "Let's try to catch one," and they pressed forward in a laughing group toward a huge seal. Undaunted, the big fellow barked sharply and kept right on flip-flopping toward the water.

"Grab him by the tail," shouted David—so they all grabbed, only to have those who held on pulled with a swish into the water.

Later they saw another great seal. A seaman called out, "Now, boys, let's show our American skill. String out, each man ready to catch hold of him." But David, not liking the seal's looks, scurried back to the boat. The animal, with a mighty roar, dashed through to the water, the men scattering to right and left as he passed.

They all laughingly accused David of being afraid.

"Perhaps, gentlemen," said David meekly. "But I never undertake anything I do not go through with."

8

Surprise Attack

MEANWHILE the crew had been busy with paint and brush disguising the ship to look like a Spanish merchantman. David observed how they painted guns where there were none, and cunningly concealed the ones they had. Then they camouflaged her lines to give the effect of a sloop.

Cruising the waters in the Galápagos region, the *Essex* didn't sight a sail; and Capatin Porter was worried. "Do you think, Mr. Downes, that the ships have been warned by the Spanish? That they may know what our business is here?"

"Sir, I doubt anyone knows of our new disguise as a Spanish merchantman," Lieutenant Downes answered. "Perhaps our luck will change."

And it did; for at sunrise on the twenty-ninth of April,

Captain Porter was awakened by the welcome cry, "Sail ho! Sail ho!"

Soon all hands were on deck, watching a large ship bearing west; and the *Essex* gave chase. "Now," thought David, "we'll have a real fight on our hands," and an hour later, when two more ships were sighted bearing southward, he was sure of it. Under English colors the *Essex* overtook the westbound vessel, the British whaler *Montezuma*, with fourteen hundred barrels of sperm oil aboard. Quickly Porter's men boarded her, surprising the unprepared crew, who put up no fight, and again David was disappointed.

Her captain and his crew were transferred to the *Essex*, and a prize crew was placed on the *Montezuma*. Then together they set out to chase the other two vessels, but by noon the wind died down.

There, only eight miles away, lay two rich prizes. David heard the prisoners say they were the *Georgiana* and the *Policy*, one with thirty-five men and the other with twenty-six. "If a breeze sprang up they could escape," he groaned. But Captain Porter had other ideas and ordered, "Get out the small boats and pull!"

Proudly David found himself at the head of the line, in charge of the oarsmen in Lieutenant Downes' boat. He stood in the stern sheets to give the time. Aiiiiiiiiiiiii-yo!" he shouted. "Eeee-aaaasssssyyy does it." Seven boats in a row followed behind. The crew sat stripped to the waist before him—two rows of six men each, stroking their oars in unison.

"Pull now, you swabs!" David called "Puuuuuuuullllll now! Put your backs to it—like Yankee men. You're in the Naaavvvv-eeeeeee!"

At his side sat Sam Riley like a statue, handling the great steering bar calmly. It looked easy, but David knew it took years to learn to handle a boat like that. If only he could take a boat through each swell the way Sam did!

But under the broiling sun even his job was tiring enough, as mile after mile they rowed. Soon David could see the strangers clearly and, from their fat lines, their trying-out vats for whale blubber, and other equipment on deck, he knew they were whalers.

It was a good three hours later before they were near enough for a line of battle. At a sign from Lieutenant Downes, David gave the command, "Way enough."

Breathing out gustily, the crew relaxed on their oars—and the boat lost its forward motion. David stood tall to give hand signals to the boats behind him, and these were repeated down the line.

The signal meant "Form a double column of attack, the odd boats falling out to form a second line." When all were in position, David raised his hand again and the boats swept forward in a new formation.

As they approached the nearest ship David blinked, not believing what he saw. Hundreds of huge turtles were swimming around it— each turtle with its head raised, straining above the water like a rocking horse. Paddling with their flippers, the creatures bobbed on the water like corks. Later David learned that the Captain, seeing the boats coming, had thrown the turtles overboard to lighten the ship. Sam Riley was having a difficult time steering through them, when "Whang!" The stranger opened fire on the Essex men. A cannon ball whistled across, sending up a spray of water all about them.

David's swarthy face paled momentarily, but as he heard the other men jeer, "Pea shooters, the fellow's got—nothing over six pounds," his fear left him.

"Those whalers shoot like farmers," laughed a brawny sailor.

"Our mate's up there now, and he'll teach them landlubbers what a gun's for!"

The enemy ship fired only once again. This time the ball whirred past and plunged into the water behind them—sending up a geyser. At the same moment she broke her flag, and the Union Jack floated down in surrender.

David's boat closed in and suddenly Lieutenant Downes stood up in the bow, raising to its full height an American flag fixed to a boarding pike. For a moment nothing happened; then a mighty cheer burst from their enemy. They waved their arms and shouted, "We are Americans aboard here!"

Grinning faces stared down, and helping hands reached out to assist Lieutenant Downes and Midshipman Farragut aboard. They found that nearly all the crew were Americans who had been pressed into British service and were happy to be freed by their own countrymen.

The second ship surrendered quickly, making three prizes in one day—worth half a million dollars! "So our hardships around the Horn have not been in vain." Captain Porter could scarcely conceal his elation. From the prizes came needed ship's articles and new supplies. Once more the Essex was overhauled and repainted to remove her disguise as a Spanish merchantman.

By June three more British whalers were captured, and midshipmen from the Essex were sent to man the prizes. David's friends William Feltus and Merry Fittimary became acting lieutenants. "If this keeps up," William announced excitedly, "we'll all be captains in no time!"

David's eyes lighted. "Patience, man," said Merry, patting the small midshipman's back. "Your chance will come."

9

Prize Master at Twelve

SEVEN prizes in a month! With so many prisoners to look after, and all in dire need of fresh water, Captain Porter made for the mouth of the Tumbez.

One of the prizes, the *Atlantic*, was large and swift; so Captain Porter armed her with ten six-pounders, ten eighteen-pounder carronades, and ammunition taken from the conquered ships. A crew of sixty was to man her, with Lieutenant Downes in command and William Kingsbury as her boatswain. Hailed by a salute of seventeen guns from the *Essex*, she was rechristened the *Essex Junior*.

David worked diligently helping Kingsbury change her over to a warship, hoping Lieutenant Downes might choose him to serve under him. With a small crew, perhaps he could act as a regular officer and not have all the petty midshipman chores to do. But

Lieutenant Downes was sternly silent, Captain Porter said nothing, and the little fleet was ready to move.

Then on the thirtieth of June the orders of the day were read: "*Midshipman Farragut transferred as Prize Master to the U.S. prize Barclay.*" Could he be hearing right? David thought. Prize Master! Not only would he have the duty of a regular officer but, actually, he would be an acting captain. He had forgotten about the *Barclay*, the American whaler captured by a privateer from Peru and retaken by the *Essex*. David knew he was chosen because there were no more officers to man her, but it was the chance he had been waiting for. He would show them what he had learned and could do in the Navy.

While he was packing his sea bag, a messenger told him Captain Porter wanted him in his cabin. Once there he saluted sharply, then noticed a huge man dressed in blue broadcloth standing behind the Captain's table. With his fierce red beard and bushy light-colored eyebrows, he looked like old Father Neptune himself.

"Mr. Farragut," said Captain Porter, "this is Captain Randall, late master of the *Barclay*." David shook hands gravely. "And now, Captain Randall," continued Captain Porter, "Mr. Farragut will be my personal representative on board the *Barclay*. He will be in command of the ship. You will be his navigating officer."

He placed his hand on David's shoulder. "I have every confidence that Mr. Farragut will do his duty as an officer. But I will appreciate your cooperation, Captain Randall. Any help you can give him out of your many years of experience at sea, I hope you'll contribute. I wish you both, gentlemen, a prosperous voyage."

"Aye, aye, Captain," the red-bearded giant said. "You can count on me for sure. I'll keep an eye on him—see that no harm comes to him on the *Barclay*."

Saluting once more, David went back to his packing. He selected Sam Riley as his boatswain and they were rowed over in state to the Barclay, with their prize crew.

There they prepared to put out to sea. Then David ate dinner with Captain Randall at his big cabin table. Later Randall pointed to one of two bunks. "Yours," he muttered through his beard, and soon was snoring in his own bunk. But David lay awake for a time, thinking over what must be done tomorrow. He was up at daylight, saluting the Essex and the ships returning with her to the Galápagos Islands.

The Barclay was one of five vessels that would follow the Essex Junior to Valparaiso, and David could see the lead ship making sail. Presently she hoisted the signal directing the other ships to follow, weighed anchor, and started out to sea.

It was now the Barclay's turn and, making his voice sound as deep as he could, David gave the order: "Stand by to man the capstan!" By the smiles of the crew, David knew they were amused at his acting as Captain; but when Sam Riley's voice boomed out a repeat of his order, they went quickly to their stations.

Ready to give the next order, David felt a heavy hand on his shoulder. Captain Randall said in a voice sharp as a knife, "Very well done, my lad. Ye sound like a sailor indade. But I'll be givin' the orders on this ship from now on."

David shrugged his hand off. "Thank you for the offer, Captain Randall," he said stiffly, "but my orders are to command this prize and I must obey them."

"Now, now, come, my little sea cock, no offense." The Captain chuckled as if it were a joke. "Ye can sit down in the cabin and play Captain as big as life, but 'tis man's work on deck. I'll just take over here and relieve ye of all responsibility and worry."

David glanced out toward the Essex Junior, but she was now beyond signaling distance. It was now or never. Maybe Captain

Randall had planned all along to get his ship back and go on with his whaling voyage, and there were enough of his men left to help him. David knew that if he gave one inch all was lost.

The sailors were waiting at the capstan bars for the next command, and he could see them grinning at one another. David's voice rang out strong and sure. "I want the topsail filled away. Follow the *Essex Junior*."

Captain Randall stepped to the rail. "This is my ship and I am master here," he bellowed. "I don't intend to trust my life to this blasted bantam, nor your lives either." He waved his hand to include the crew.

There was but one thing to do, and David stepped forward. "Mr. Riley, I want the anchor weighed immediately. Set the fore and mainsails, and"—here David looked up as if he were judging the breeze and weather, but really to swallow the lump in his throat—"I want that topsail filled away! We will follow the *Essex Junior* without further delay."

Captain Randall's face grew red as his beard and he raised his hamlike fist to bring it down on the rail with a crash. "I'll shoot the first man who moves his hand on this ship without my orders," he bellowed.

David pressed his hands to the rail tightly to hide their trembling. "Weigh anchor, Mr. Riley," he commanded. "I have Captain Porter's orders."

Sam Riley hesitated only a second; then, like the sun, a grin spread over his face. "Aye, aye, sir," he said delightedly as he saluted. He cupped his hands and roared, "Step lively, there. Weigh anchor! Put some beef into it, my hearties, and wipe those grins off. You've heard your orders."

Then he lifted his deep bass voice to sing "Blow the Man Down," and the sailors joined in. Their cheerful voices rang out as they gave a mighty heave on the capstan bars, and David drew a deep breath.

Blurting out an oath, Captain Randall rushed down the hatch. "I'll show ye," he roared, beside himself with fury.

David was no longer frightened; his men had obeyed him. He stood by the hatch, and as Randall came into view he shouted, "Stand back! Captain Randall, stand back! If you set foot on deck with those pistols, you'll go overboard!

"Mr. Riley," sang out David, "detail two men aft. If Captain Randall appears on the quarter-deck, throw him overboard."

Two husky seamen appeared beside David, spitting on their hands and rubbing them together hopefully. Not often could a seaman boast that he had thrown a captain overboard. More burly sailors gathered behind David, who stood ramrod-straight with lips tight and face set.

Captain Randall stared at him; then at Sam Riley, and all the grim sailors backing their young Captain. Toss a skipper into the Pacific? Yes, they looked as if they would enjoy that. Randall thrust his pistols into his greatcoat pockets and, muttering, withdrew down the hatch. No doubt now who was in command of the Barclay.

David made haste to catch up with the squadron. For two days and nights he shared the cabin with Randall, without speaking. On the third day Randall tried to joke with him; but David refused to answer, fearing a trick.

When the Barclay was able to bring up alongside the Essex Junior, David hastened to report to Lieutenant Downes, ordering Captain Randall to go with him. As he finished his report, the Lieutenant turned on the red-bearded man in anger. "And what explanation have you to offer for your conduct, Captain Randall?"

" 'Twas nothin', Sir," the Captain laughed. "Only a joke from an old sea dog to a young 'un. Just wanted to see if he frightened easy."

"Ask him, sir," insisted David, angry now, "how well he succeeded."

"Nay. I only meant it as a joke—to show the lad the way of the sea." The Captain was floundering now.

Lieutenant Downes stared at him. "I don't believe your explanation. You are under Navy command, and such jokes are not tolerated. Any like report in the future and you'll be put in irons."

Captain Randall backed out fast and, when he was gone, Lieutenant Downes smiled at David, then grew serious. "That fellow was trying to get hold of the ship, wasn't he?"

"Yes, sir, he was."

"Um-m. Rather a rough customer. Would you like me to send someone else to the *Barclay?*"

David was panic-stricken—to lose his command when he had just proved he could handle it! "Oh, no, sir! Please do not, sir!" he pleaded.

"Then shall I keep Captain Randall aboard with me to be sure he makes no more trouble?" Lieutenant Downes asked.

"No, sir," replied David. "I—my crew and I can handle him, sir." Pride in his men showed in his voice.

"Very well, Mr. Farragut." Lieutenant Downes smiled again. "You have behaved with initiative and resolution. I will see that Captain Porter receives a report of this matter. By the way, how old are you?"

David was surprised at this question and started to say "Eleven." Then he saw on Lieutenant Downes' wall calendar in large letters: JULY 5.

"I am twelve years old, sir—today."

"Indeed? Very well. Congratulations. Resume command of the

Barclay, Mr. Farragut." David sensed by the tone of the Lieutenant's voice that he was pleased with him.

David returned to his ship without delay. Randall and he never became friendly, but nothing more happened between them while the *Barclay* held her course for Valparaiso.

David had accomplished something no one else in the history of the Navy or the Merchant Marine had ever done: *achieved command of a ship at the age of twelve!*

10

Nuku Hiva—Lost Paradise

THE *Essex Junior* returned to the Galápagos Islands with the officers and men from the prizes, and once more David was a midshipman. While at Valparaiso he had heard news which he now relayed to Captain Porter. "England is sending a superior force to the Pacific to destroy our American whalers and capture the *Essex!*"

"They shall find us ready and waiting when they arrive," Captain Porter stated calmly. "Meanwhile we've added four more whalers to our fleet. There's only one left around here and she's laid up in some port."

"That means our work as a commerce destroyer in these waters is finished, sir," remarked Lieutenant Downes, pleased.

"Aye," agreed the Captain. "We've completely broken British whale fishing on the coast of Chile and Peru. The loss to our enemy is two and a half million dollars. She has also lost the services of three hundred and sixty seamen released on parole. Now we'll sail farther west to hide, while we refit for battle."

So on October the second the *Essex Junior*, with the *Essex* and her prizes, dropped anchor in the quiet harbor of Nuku Hiva on the Marquesas. Some of these islands showed steep cliffs of black volcanic rock, some the rich green of vegetation; in others, cascades tumbled from the mountains. To David, even the heavy shower clouds which rolled up in big masses looked beautiful; and when the sun came through, everything appeared more glorious than before.

When the natives got over their fear of the strangers, they came paddling out in eight canoes filled with coconuts and fruits to trade, repeating the word *tanya* (friend). At a distance they had appeared to David to be dressed in close-fitting tights, heavily ornamented. But when they came aboard he saw that their bodies were almost completely tattooed, the patterns circling out from the joints.

Their chief, Gattanewa, was very friendly and invited them ashore. The native houses were grouped on the hillsides of Nuku Hiva overlooking the bay. David and the boys found clear fresh streams in the valley, which was carpeted with velvety lawns and so thickly covered with luxuriant groves of tropical fruit-bearing trees that few houses could be seen. They discovered coconut trees, many different kinds of bananas, and sugar cane that grew higher than the tallest man among them.

But the natives liked best the breadfruit tree. Planted in groves, its large, spreading leaves reminded David of his fig tree in New Orleans. The oval fruit looked like a big round loaf of bread; the natives served it baked, boiled, or roasted, and the Americans found it delicious. From the bark of its small branches the natives made cloth, and from the trunk of the tree their long graceful canoes and carven images of their gods.

Gattanewa, chief of the Taeehs, the tribe which lived near the bay of Nuku Hiva, was much pleased when Captain Porter gave him a whale's tooth, for it was prized even more than jewels. David learned that ten whale's teeth could buy three hundred tons of sandalwood, which would bring nearly a million dollars when sold in China!

In return the chief helped Captain Porter set up a camp on shore, and carpenter, cooper, sailmaker, and blacksmith shops were set up where repairs on the Essex could be made. The barricade surrounding it was guarded by marines, and each day, until four in the afternoon, the men worked on sails, spars, and gear. After eleven months at sea the Essex needed a thorough overhauling.

Greatly impressed by the marching of the marines, the sound of drums, and the firing of muskets, Gattanewa asked Captain Porter for help to fight the Happahs, a mountain tribe making raids into his valley.

"Mr. Farragut," said Captain Porter, "we'll bring ashore a six-pounder if his men will carry it to the top of the mountain; then our gunners will drive the Happahs from the hills."

To the Captain's surprise the natives hauled the gun up to the mountaintop in a matter of hours. "Now," David announced, "you've got to keep your promise."

Downes led the attack, and in the skirmish the Happahs lost five men and Lieutenant Downes none. Within two days envoys from all the tribes on the islands, except the Typees, came to make peace on Porter's terms.

His only demand was, "Live at peace together. Bring me what supplies I need. I'll pay with iron hoops, hooks, pigs, or whatever you need."

Several days later David ran to Porter to point out a strange procession of four thousand natives from different tribes bringing materials with them. By night they had built a house for the

Captain, another for the officers, a sail loft, a place for the sick, a bakehouse, a guardhouse, and even a shelter for the sentinel to walk under.

"That's true gratitude, my boy," Captain Porter exclaimed to David after Gattanewa had explained that the settlement was for the Americans to live in while repairing the ship.

And Merry remarked to David as they moved ashore, "Well, we won't have to fight off the rats tonight with our belaying pins."

"And glad I am," agreed David, his beaked nose wrinkling. "I'm tired of finding rats everywhere I turn."

So the first job, before loading the powder and good provisions on the ships, was to smoke out with charcoal the fifteen hundred or so rats aboard the Essex.

Afterward carpenters and sailmakers, with the help of the natives, replaced the decayed topmast. Painting and calking had to be done and the natives were a great help here, too; for they were expert divers and could work under water. They helped also to scrape off barnacles and repair the copper sheathing on the hull.

Once the Essex was shipshape again, the midshipmen returned aboard; for Captain Porter did not want the easy island life to soften his crew. He reminded them that they were at sea to become officers and not for a good time, and that they must acquire rigid discipline for sea fighting.

Again the chaplain, Mr. Adams, set up school on the Essex. "Imagine," thought David, "being in the mysterious and exotic South Seas and studying geography, spelling, and arithmetic cooped up on ship as you would be back home in school." If the boys' attention strayed, Mr. Adams was sharp with them. "Eyes on your book, please!" he would snap severely.

But, having stood watch for long months, they found problems of navigation easier; and the strange names of foreign ports, once they had visited them, were less difficult to remember. Then a glimpse of the beach through an open porthole would set them to daydreaming, and Mr. Adams' voice would be stern.

"Mr. Feltus, eyes front and sit erect there; Henry Ogden, give your attention, or your leave from the ship will be forfeited this afternoon." At this all eyes would be glued to the books; for no one wanted to miss going ashore, especially David. He had made friends with Tamaha, Gattanewa's son.

Tamaha had taught David to swim, and shown him the tricky knack of throwing the long fish spear. As the tide came in, he would spear the fish in the surf.

David was amazed at the Taeeh mothers who walked out into the deep water with their babies—often no more than two years old—on their backs. There they left them to themselves, and he laughed every time he saw the babies come in paddling like ducks.

One day as David, Merry, and Henry Ogden came ashore they noticed the natives on a hillside. "What are they doing?" asked Henry. "I can't make it out."

David saw them raise their right arms and then let them fall sharply. "Let's go see," he said, his spine tingling. As they came closer, he smiled. He had guessed right: the Nuku Hivans were practicing slinging. He didn't say anything, but once again he was back at Stony Point with his brother Will showing him how to sling.

Here on the island the native boys were using coconuts in a grove near the beach as targets. Their slings were made from fibers of the coconut tree, and David noticed they hurled quite large stones. "Hooray!" he cheered as Tamaha made one perfect shot after another. Then he asked to borrow his sling.

Feeling the motion of it, David raised his arm and let his stone fly with sure force toward the grove; and everyone saw the coconut fall to the ground.

"Well, I'll be blowed!" cried Merry.

"Where did you learn that?" demanded Ogden.

Tamaha saluted David in native fashion with outstretched arm, and from then on he was even more particularly David's friend.

Now all the other midshipmen wanted to try the sling. David, however, took no chances with his luck. He *told* them how, but he did not try to *show* them how to sling!

From Tamaha, David learned the native tongue—and also came to understand what each line of tattooing meant. Tamaha already had bands on his wrists and ankles and he was very proud of them, for he was only seventeen years old. Tattooing was so painful that most youths did not begin until they were at least eighteen, and a man seldom was completely tattooed before he was thirty-five.

David was much interested in the warriors who thronged the American village, colorful in their plumes made of the feathers of cocks and man-of-war birds. They wore long red or white cloaks of feathers, and ornaments of whale teeth or ivory dangled from their ears or hung about their necks. They carried black, highly polished spears twelve feet long, while some had richly carved clubs.

They had come to tell Captain Porter that the Typees refused to be friends with the Taeehs and Americans. They had called the white chief and his men "white lizards." They might attack.

"Gattanewa," said Captain Porter, "get your warriors ready, and tell the Happahs to bring their war canoes. We will protect the village." He sent his men to build breastworks on top of the hill near by, and mounted four guns.

But David, Merry, and the other midshipmen were disappointed; for although they had helped haul and mount the guns and bring ammunition, they were not taken on the fighting expedition. From the ship's rail they watched the warriors, armed with slings, spears, and shields, set out with the seamen for the bay of the Typees.

The next day the thirty-five men returned carrying Lieutenant Downes, who had suffered a broken leg. "We barely escaped with our lives," said Captain Porter. "We'll need more men." So on the following day two hundred men went over the mountain, the seamen armed with cutlasses and swords.

"Hope Will Kingsbury keeps his eyes and ears open," David said to Merry.

"Whatever happens, he'll make a good story of it anyway," grinned Merry.

Three days later the war party trooped back and Kingsbury described the battle. "David, you never saw fighting like that," he said, shaking his head.

"Where were you?" asked David.

"On a plateau with Porter's men. The Happahs were on the other side of it. The drums rolled, and one warrior from our side danced out a ways toward the enemy—kind of daring them, see? They waited for him to get well out into the open, then the enemy threw stones and spears at him."

"Stones?"

"Whoppers, some half a pound. Then," Kingsbury went on, excitedly demonstrating, "our warrior-dancer wriggled and turned about—like this—so's to miss the stones. Next the spears were flying at him; so he danced back, with the Typees fast on his heels. Then Gattanewa and *his* men ran down to meet them, and the Happas came out of hiding and they all met in a little fancy fightin'."

"So what did you do?"

"We watched it awhile, then fired a few shots in the air—and you should have seen their faces! The Typees were too scared to run."

"And then?" persisted David.

"That was the end of the war!" laughed Kingsbury.

Days of feasting followed to celebrate the victory. In war regalia the chiefs came over the hills to make peace on any terms with Captain Porter, driving a thousand hogs as a peace offering to the Americans.

Next day David held in his hands the Stars and Stripes as they were raised over the fort, and a salute of seventeen guns was fired from its cannon. The ships in the harbor returned the salute.

David felt a thrill of pride as Captain Porter read: "I, David Porter, Captain in the American Navy, take possession of these islands, known as the Marquesas, in the name of the United States and rename them *Madison* in honor of the President of my country." As the sailors cheered, the natives beat their breasts and cried, "Melleekees! Melleekees!"—meaning they, too, were "Americans" now.

Soon afterward the *Essex* was fully refitted and armed, and Porter left his prizes at Nuku Hiva in charge of selected officers and men. The *Essex* and the *Essex Junior* were ready to sail—and to wait at Valparaiso for the enemy British, who were bound to stop there after rounding Cape Horn.

When the natives heard Captain Porter was departing, Tamaha came in a canoe to say good-bye, bringing a little red pig called "Far-o-gee" (his affectionate name for David).

"Thank you, Tamaha; but I shall call him Murphy," David said, "after the redheaded Irishman we have aboard."

"Mor-phee," nodded Tamaha, smiling, as David gave him an iron fishhook, valued above all other gifts by the islanders.

"Come back, Far-o-gee. Come back again to Nuku Hiva," Tamaha called as he pushed off in his canoe.

"I will, Tamaha. I will." David waved. "Fare you well."

Last Fight of the "Essex"

EARLY in February, 1814, the American vessels reentered the harbor of Valparaiso. The voyage had been uneventful; but the men had been drilled for every emergency, working with pikes, belaying pins, grappling irons, small arms, and the great guns. And the midshipmen, like David, were well trained as boarders, with pistol, dirk, cutlass, and swords. The *Essex Junior* was stationed at the entrance to signal the approach of any ship resembling a British man-of-war.

Finding no sign of the enemy, Captain Porter gave a great ball on the *Essex* for the Governor, his officials, and their ladies. After midnight the midshipmen on watch took down the gay decorations of red, white, and blue bunting. David was still too young for the dance, but he listened to William Feltus and Henry Ogden talk about the gay señoritas.

Gazing across the harbor at the Essex Junior, David suddenly saw her signals. "Look, Will, the Essex Junior is talking to us."

Together they slowly spelled out the lights. "T-w-o e-n-e-m-y s-h-i-p-s s-t-a-n-d-i-n-g w-i-t-h t-h-e w-i-n-d t-o t-h-e s-o-u-t-h-w-a-r-d."

"Holy smoke!" cried Will, but David was already halfway down to report to Captain Porter. Checking on the signals, the Captain ordered a gun fired to recall all men on liberty ashore.

Morning showed the two ships to be the English thirty-six-gun frigate Phoebe—commanded by Captain James Hillyard, whom Captain Porter had known many years before on the Mediterranean—and the eighteen-gun sloop Cherub.

The Essex Junior anchored and stood by the Essex; both ships lay within the three-mile limit, the neutral zone safe from attack. On came the two ships till the Phoebe was within fifteen feet of the Essex, and it looked for a minute as if their yardarms would foul. Every man on the Essex was at his battle station; the gun-ports were triced up, and the tampions removed from the muzzles of the guns. The powder boys held their slow-burning long gun matches, blowing on them to keep them glowing red-hot. Boarders gripped their sharp cutlasses and pikes, ready to leap through the smoke and grapple with the enemy.

Suddenly David heard the boy at the gun beside him cry out. One of the Phoebe's crew was sneering at them through a port-hole, and making foul remarks about American courage.

"I'll show you!" the boy shouted, jumping forward to light his gun. Lieutenant McKnight promptly knocked him down.

If that gun had been fired, the Essex could have captured the Phoebe. But, instead, when Captain Hillyar saw the Essex ready for action he hailed, "Captain Hillyar's compliments to Captain Porter, and his hopes that he is well."

"Very well, thank you," shouted Captain Porter, "and kindly

keep a proper distance. An accident might prove disagreeable."

Captain Hillyar hastily altered sail. "If I do fall athwart you, I assure you it will be entirely accidental!" he shouted back.

Captain Porter retorted, "You have no business where you are. If you touch a timber of this ship, I shall board instantly."

As the *Phoebe* retreated, her jib boom passed over a portion of the *Essex's* deck; but no harm was done. Because of his respect for the neutrality of the port, Captain Porter withheld his fire when he could easily have taken the enemy vessel. His high sense of honor won him fame the world over, but it was to cost him his ship!

The *Phoebe* and the *Cherub* anchored just outside the harbor to block the port; and time and again one or the other would run in close to the *Essex*, then veer off at the last moment—with a shot fired out to sea. Captain Porter knew it as an old trick to lure him out into battle with the two ships. One he could handle; two could outmaneuver him, David understood.

So for six weeks the *Essex* was bottled up in port, the crew and officers angry at the futility of answering the challenges. Captain Porter then received news that three more ships had sailed in search of him, and that the *Raccoon*, the third vessel in the *Phoebe's* squadron, was coming in to help her. All those ships could trap him here for the rest of the war. Captain Porter decided to run the blockade, taking his chances, under the gale then blowing, to gain the open sea.

Suddenly a heavy squall struck the *Essex*, jamming the main topgallant yard and tossing the frigate almost on her beam ends. Then the main topmast crashed; and David knew that now the Captain could not outsail his enemies, nor could he get back to the harbor. He dropped anchor in a small cove half a mile from shore.

A shout came from the lookout, and David saw the Phoebe and the Cherub bearing down on them in battle array.

The crew of the Essex sprang to battle stations as Fittimary shouted, "They're taking advantage of our crippled ship while we're in a neutral zone!"

David, on the quarter-deck as aide to Captain Porter, stared at the men around him. Their strained faces showed they were ready to fight and die, though they knew their position was hopeless.

The Phoebe touched off a broadside, and with a roar the battle was on. The first shots fell short, sending up spray as they struck the water. The British ships had long-range guns, and made sure not to get close enough for the Essex to use her deadly carronades. The Essex had only three guns to carry for distance, but these did so much damage that the English had to withdraw to repair their cut rigging.

Porter daringly decided to close in on them, but the wind shifted and he could not do this. Then he tried to haul his ship around on a hawser bent to the anchor cable, but a cannon ball cut it in two. From then on everything went wrong.

David ran all kinds of errands, helped the powder boys serving the guns, and ran back and forth with orders. Once his friend Feltus reported to the Captain, "Sir, a quarter gunner, Roach, has deserted his post."

Porter turned to David and handed him a loaded pistol. "Do your duty, Mr. Farragut!" he said grimly.

David took the pistol, knowing he would have to shoot the deserter; then to his immense relief he learned, when he got below, that the coward had taken a boat and disappeared.

When David first saw a seaman killed by a cannon ball, he vomited; but soon he was so busy he had no time to feel or think —he could only act. There were so many wounded that buckets of sand were scattered on the decks where the blood made them slippery. Once when he was sent below for gun primers, he reached the ladder just as one of the gun crew directly across the hatch was mangled by a round shot. The body was flung against him and the two fell down the hatch. David picked himself up, his breath knocked out of him, and hurried back to the deck.

Captain Porter saw David's torn and bloody clothes and asked, "Are you wounded, Mr. Farragut?"

"No, sir," he answered stoutly.

"Then where are the primers?" demanded Porter. David had clean forgotten them, and rushed to get them. When he returned he found the Captain lying down, and it was his turn to ask, "Are you wounded, sir?"

And the Captain's answer was, "No, I believe not." A cannon ball had passed so close to his head that the concussion had crushed his hat and knocked him flat.

The batteries of the two enemy ships pounded the *Essex* steadily for two hours, and David watched the men trying to repair rigging and plug up holes while they kept the guns firing. Finally Captain Porter saw it was hopeless and ordered the ship run aground, to destroy her.

Suddenly a huge explosion in the hold shook the *Essex* as if she were cardboard, and smoke and flames burst from the hatch. Men came running up with their clothes aflame; and Porter commanded them to jump overboard and try to swim to shore, which some did.

Others stayed, trying to control the fire; but all was over now and Captain Porter ordered the colors hauled down. After two and a half hours of furious resistance the *Essex* had to surrender; yet for ten minutes after this, Captain Hillyar kept firing—killing four men by Captain Porter's side!

David had one last errand to do. "Quickly, before they come

aboard!" Captain Porter called. "Find the signal book and destroy it."

David ran to the Captain's cabin and, though he searched everywhere, he could not find the code book. When he thought of the enemy's taking the *Essex*, his first ship, he became so angry that tears burned his eyes, blinding him momentarily. Shaking his head, he thought wildly, "Where is that book? The enemy must not find the secret signals."

Hurrying to the gun deck, he saw Fittimary. "I can't find the code book. Have you seen it?"

"Seems to me Lieutenant McKnight had it last, but I'll help you look."

They made their way over the slippery deck and stumbled over the mangled bodies of their comrades, searching everywhere. Then David saw the book on the sill of a gun port. He snatched it up in a flood of relief. "We must get rid of it. Throw it overboard," he said. "Weight it down some way."

Merry hurried off and came back with a heavy chain which they wound round and round, snapping the links tight.

"There! That should do it," David said, and flung the signal book overboard. They watched it sink out of sight. Then the two went through the wardrooms, collecting pistols and firearms which they also tossed overboard so that they would not fall into the hands of the enemy as trophies.

David fingered the dirk at his side. He slid it from its sheath and caressed its shining blade. "Merry, I won't give up my dirk. The armorer made it from a file just for me."

"I know," Merry nodded. "But perhaps only the Captain will be forced to give up his dirk when they come aboard."

"Let's chuck ours overboard. I'd rather do that and make certain they don't get them." So both dropped their dirks overside, watching them flash as they sank into the sea.

They found Will Feltus standing by the mizzenmast supporting himself with one hand; he had been struck by a huge splinter and carried overboard. His clothes were soaked and his face was pale, but he was not seriously injured. Kingsbury, however, was badly hurt, and for some time after was out of his head with fever and suffering from his severe burns.

That night the British took possession of the *Essex*, and the next morning David, as a prisoner of war, was taken aboard the *Phoebe*. Below, in the steerage, he sat head in hand, miserable over the loss of his ship and many friends.

Presently he looked up to see an English reefer come running with a small pig in his arms. "A prize, a prize!" he shouted. "A fine grunter, by Jove."

David recognized Murphy, *his* pet pig! His own gift from Tamaha! Forgetting his tears, he jumped up shouting, "Here, that's mine! Put him down!"

"Ho! But you are a prisoner of war; so is this pig," retorted the English boy.

"In our Navy we always respect private property," David said angrily, and grabbed one of Murphy's legs. "Put him down; he's mine!" he insisted.

"Go to it, little Yankee," urged one of the other English boys. "If you can thrash Shorty, you shall have your pig."

"Agreed," shouted David, letting go of the pig and whipping off his jacket. Remembering that the English believed in fair play, he knew he would have a good chance to get his pig back.

Quickly a ring formed around the two boys and they went at each other with bare fists. Shorty had plenty of fight and wind, but he was no match for David's well-trained fists and light, quick feet. Besides, David's determination to get his pet back added the extra power to his punch. When Shorty at last cried "Enough! Enough!" David picked up his coat and tucked

Murphy under his arm. He felt good. Somehow, winning over the English boy helped to make up for the loss of his ship. Anyway he felt considerably better.

The prisoners from the Essex were paroled and put ashore on their word of honor not to fight in the war again until they had been exchanged for English prisoners. A house was found for the wounded where the ladies of Valparaiso nursed them, saving many lives.

David offered his help. Up at dawn every morning, he laid out fresh bandages; then after breakfast he spent long days helping the surgeons. The wounded liked having him around and looked for his cheery face.

At the end of April, 1814, the Essex Junior carried the survivors home to the States, and on that long voyage David continued to care for the injured. Of the original two hundred and fifty-five officers and men who went into battle that fateful day, only one hundred and thirty-two, including the wounded, were left.

In New York the crew was welcomed enthusiastically, for stories of the glorious Essex had preceded their arrival. The crowd unhitched the horses from Captain Porter's carriage and drew him through the streets to his lodging, David sharing with him the gratitude of the people.

Meanwhile Porter had sent in his official report of the cruise of the Essex in her last battle. In it he praised his officers and men for their courage and devotion to duty during that hopeless last stand of the ship.

Among those singled out for praise was Midshipman Farragut. Captain Porter would have recommended him for promotion except for his "tender years." While he had earned the right to be made a lieutenant as far as bravery, loyalty to duty, and service went, David was still too young.

As Porter's report was reprinted far and wide by the newspapers, a copy fell into the hands of George Farragut, living on his plantation on the Pascagoula River. He read and reread that account until the paper was in shreds, and each time he showed it to neighbors he would say proudly, "See that? That's my boy!"

Yes, at thirteen David was a veteran of the seas.

12

Mediterranean Cruise

SINCE David's name had not been checked off against a British midshipman who had been captured by the Americans, Porter sent him to his home at Chester, Pennsylvania. Here, while waiting to be exchanged, he studied under an odd fellow named Neif. Once a celebrated guard of Napoleon Bonaparte, Neif drilled the boys like soldiers and taught them French.

Five months later David was exchanged and, now off parole, he gladly joined Will Ogden. Both were assigned to the brig *Spark*, which was to sail with a squadron of small vessels commanded by Captain Porter. But the brig was not ready; so the boys were quartered on the receiving ship *John Adams*, stationed in New York harbor.

"I didn't waste time in Chester," David told Will. "I learned a lot."

"When will you use it?" Will Ogden asked.

"Well, sometime that military drilling and the French I learned will come in handy," nodded David.

Aboard the *John Adams*, David spent the worst winter of his life; for it was intensely cold and there was no way to keep the steerage warm. The middies were only half-clad, and many tried to keep warm by drinking hard liquor.

For the first time David was not under the kindly eye of his foster father. He was only thirteen and, since he was the youngest, he felt he had to show he could hold his liquor like a man. Will Ogden scolded him, "David, why do you imitate these wild young men?"

Angry and ashamed, he defended himself. "What do we get to eat? Scotch coffee sweetened with molasses, and our ration for dinner."

One day Lieutenant William Cocke called David into his cabin. "Mr. Farragut, I don't like what you are doing," he said.

"I attend to my duties, sir."

"Yes, your strict attention to your assigned tasks is commendable. But how long will you be able to execute them if you continue to drink like the rest of this wild lot? Would Captain Porter be proud of your conduct? He has always spoken of you with respect, with pride. Would he now?"

David was aghast. Was that the way he looked to others? He must not let Captain Porter see him so, or even hear about him. "You are right, sir. What a fool I've been!" he said. "You won't need to worry about me again, Lieutenant Cocke"—and, saluting trimly, he left the cabin with his head held high.

David saw no further action in the war; for soon, with the Treaty of Ghent at Christmas, 1814, peace was declared, and now he was ready for new adventures.

During the war with England the Pasha of Algiers had been

demanding bigger annual tributes of ships plying his waters, and he had dared lay hands on American merchantmen. Congress declared war on him and ordered two squadrons to bring the pirate Pasha to terms—one squadron under Decatur, the other under Bainbridge. David was to serve under Bainbridge on the new ship *Independence*, the pride of the Navy.

Decatur reached Algiers first and gave his historic ultimatum to the Pasha with the muzzles of his guns; so by the time the *Independence* arrived, peace had been made. Even so, David learned that the appearance of Bainbridge's squadron, so soon after Decatur's, impressed the Barbary ruler with the sea might of the United States.

David, writing in his journal, noted: "On this trip I made the friendship of Midshipman Taylor, one of the finest officers of his rank. Older than I am, he took me in charge, advised and inspired me with sentiments of manliness. Never having any real love for dissipation," he concluded, "I easily got rid of the bad influences which had assailed me on the ship *John Adams*."

In May, 1816, David was appointed aide to Captain John Orde Creighton of the *Washington*, which was to sail to the Mediterranean as the flagship for the American squadron in those waters.

Stopping at Annapolis, Maryland, to pick up the envoy to Naples, the Honorable William Pinkney, the *Washington* was honored by a visit from President Madison. With him came members of his cabinet and other guests—among them Mr. Porter, now appointed Commodore.

David had been sent ashore with the market boat and, returning with his purchases, he made a dash below to change into full dress; but someone had pitched his sea chest into the hold. Everyone else was magnificently arrayed in lofty cocked hats, gold braid and epaulets, white trousers and shiny boots. David looked down at his shabby work clothes and, trying to keep out of sight, ducked behind the mast, the big wheel, or any big brother officer who would shield him. Several times he caught Commodore Porter's reproving eye, but he could not get close enough to explain. When President Madison finally left, David uttered a relieved "Whew!"

Though the passage to Gibraltar, lasting twenty-two days, was pleasant, David learned how disagreeable a captain can be to his men. Captain Creighton was known as a martinet in the Navy, and his *Washington* was a "crack ship"—which meant the decks shone with "spit and polish." The men made and furled sail in record time; the ship glistened, but at the expense and comfort of the crew.

To speed work aloft, the last man down got a rope laid across his shoulders; and in their haste the sailors sometimes fell and broke their legs or even their necks. But the Captain remained unmoved by such mishaps.

Often the officer of the deck called up the whole watch and gave them two or three dozen lashes apiece for the fault of one man. David most dreaded the times all hands were kept on deck all night for several nights in succession.

After this experience he told another midshipman, "When I have a ship of my own, I'll never have a crack ship—not if it means inhumanity to my men." He thought of his days with Captain Porter. "My foster father was strict, but kind. With him we always had a happy ship."

For the next few years David's duty kept him in the Mediterranean, where, always eager to learn, he took a keen interest in people he met and places he visited. On this cruise the squadron touched at various ports where the crew had a chance to go ashore. Sometimes they visited historic ruins or beautiful cathedrals and palaces, and David was quick to pick up different languages.

As aide to the flag captain he went ashore to all official entertainments, dressed in tail coat, tall cocked hat, and a dirk at his side. Standing beside his captain, he had to act as interpreter in Italian, Spanish, and French; and when the dignitaries came aboard the *Washington*, he translated for them.

He liked the Bay of Naples, where at the Bath of Nero he could lower eggs in a basket three hundred feet below the surface and have the waters of the hot springs boil them quickly. David, describing this in his journal, said: "The whole vicinity felt as if it rested on a hot furnace. When we went bathing, just digging a little in the sand on the beach, we could feel the heat."

Often the officers would seek out the arsenals in the seaport towns and fence. Since David was small he seized every opportunity to increase his skill in sports to keep up with his brother officers, whom he often beat at sword play—his special hobby.

On this cruise David made a lifelong friend—Charles Folsom, the chaplain and schoolteacher. When Folsom was appointed consul at Tunis and was about to leave the ship, he said, "How would you like to leave the squadron and live ashore for a few months, David?"

By now David was sixteen; he had no fortune or family to fall back on, and he knew that he would have to depend on himself to get ahead. He had studied hard with his chaplain.

"With you, sir?" David asked eagerly.

"Yes," said Folsom, waving an official-looking paper. "My request for your stay with me in Tunis has been granted."

"I'd like that, sir," answered David.

"Oh, you'll have a strict program of studies—French and Italian, English literature, history, and mathematics."

"I won't mind that," David said.

"But we'll have fun, too, exploring the back country, when our studies are done," Folsom promised.

So it proved. On one excursion nine days out of Tunis, they came to the ruins of El Jem, a village built from the crumbling fragments of a mighty amphitheater. It was the hottest day David had ever experienced and, since he was the youngest in the group, he had to ride in the saddle. For protection he had a large straw hat on his head and another on his back. But the rays of the sun seemed to go right through him. By late afternoon he suffered a sunstroke which paralyzed him for hours and nauseated him.

Their camp that night was among Bedouins who looked upon Christians as dogs—if they killed a Christian, they went to bed happy in having done their good deed for the day. But that night David was so miserable he didn't care what happened.

Soon afterward the plague broke out in Tunis, and Consul Folsom advised David to leave. So, after nine months, he went on to Messina, Sicily, to join the squadron.

In the spring of 1819 he made another cruise to Gibraltar, as acting lieutenant on the *Spark*, and a year later he was sent home to take his examinations for promotion to a lieutenancy. Since there was no man-of-war returning to the United States, he was dispatched with two invalided seamen on a small merchantman, the *America*.

When the ship was a few days' sail from home, a suspicious-looking stranger was sighted—flying a Colombian flag. Both vessels were becalmed, but soon a smaller boat with long oars approached the *America*. This paralyzed the Captain with fright. "It's a pirate! I know it!" he cried.

The officers of the *America* appealed to Farragut. "Take off your uniform! There's no telling what they will do with us if they see it."

"I will do nothing of the kind," Farragut answered. "We'll meet them prepared to repel boarders!" And eighteen-year-old

David promptly took charge. "Call all hands!" His voice rang with authority.

As the crew assembled on deck, the two invalided bluejackets stepped forward and saluted, "You can count on us, sir."

"I knew I could. How about it, men? How about the rest of you?" he asked.

He saw the men glance at their cringing officers, at the two sailors standing at attention, and then at him. "Aye, aye, sir," they answered—and then, all together, "We'll fight, sir!"

"Good!" said David. "We'll give the stranger a welcome he won't expect."

All he could find to fight with, however, was a heavy grindstone and a barrel of tar. These were rigged up so they could be quickly dropped over the side and through the bottom of any boat that came close in an attempted boarding.

Then a hail was heard in Spanish announcing that the crew of the boat was coming aboard with an officer. David asked in English, "Do you come as a friend?"

"Yes," came the answer, also in English.

"Leave all your arms in your boat before you come aboard!" warned David.

When the man in charge came on deck he was not a bearded pirate at all, but an American gentleman from Baltimore! He wanted the America to take a bundle of letters back to the States, and offered to supply her with anything she might need.

When he left, David burst into laughter. "What an ending to our expected fight to the death with pirates!"

The men laughed with him. David once more had shown he could take over in an emergency, and command. He had learned that "men trained to arms will never fail, if properly led."

13

Hunting Pirates in the Caribbean

WHEN David reported to New York to take his examinations for the grade of lieutenant, he was afraid he might not pass in mathematics; but, with his experience at sea, he felt certain he would qualify in seamanship. His cruise record was excellent; his superior officers all had given him high rating, even the exacting Commodore Creighton. But when he took his examinations, he learned that a "man's personal qualifications will not bear himself against his superiors."

Earlier David had been heard to say that Raymond Perry (brother of Commodore Oliver H. Perry) was a drunkard. Though this officer was called to face court-martial, his brother-in-law, Captain G. W. Rodgers, challenged David, accusing him of circulating "injurious rumors." David told him, "Captain, when you lay aside your official rank and meet me as a friend of Mr. Perry, I shall be glad to settle all difficulties between him and myself."

This was a mistake; a middy was expected to be meek and humble before his superior officers. When David came up before the examiners, Captain Samuel Evan, a friend of Rodgers, considered David a "most insubordinate young man" who needed to be taught a lesson.

During the examinations as David was telling what to do in reefing topsails, this officer snarled, "You neglected to clear away your bowlines."

Trying hard to control himself, David answered, "You must not have heard me, sir, but I certainly did. I have had too much experience in reefing topsails not to know that much."

Evan swore furiously. "You insolent puppy, contradicting your superiors!" he shouted.

When the three examiners met to pass on David, he was failed. Feeling unjustly treated, he wrote with bitterness in his journal: "It was the hardest blow I have ever sustained to my pride and the greatest mortification to my vanity." He had expected a rebuke, but a punishment that was to hound him during his life he felt was most unfair.

In July, 1821, David again took the examinations and by October was writing a friend: "I aimed at the head but was glad to catch at number 26 out of 53." Instead of an immediate promotion to the rank of lieutenant, his name was merely added to the list of "Midshipmen Passed for Promotion" eligible when a vacancy occurred.

He still drew only midshipman's pay—nineteen dollars a month! By the time he had paid his mess bills and kept up his uniforms, there was not much left with which to help support his sisters. And now there was the "One and Only" young and charming lady in Norfolk who had consoled him when he failed his examinations before.

Then David was sent to the *John Adams* to escort Minister Joel Poinsett to Mexico. The trip took five months, during which David gained valuable knowledge of the Mexican coast, an insight into the character of the Mexicans, and practiced his Spanish. So at twenty-one he had added another four thousand miles to his sea record.

Not long afterward he was transferred to Commodore Porter's "Mosquito Fleet," the squadron sent to rid the West Indies of pirates. While the Spanish colonies were revolting against Spain, buccaneers masquerading under the flags of South American countries were preying on American merchantmen.

When he embarked on the *Greyhound*, David thought that fighting pirates would be just an exciting adventure; but he found it dangerous and difficult. The buccaneers would not fight a pitched battle, but ran and hid in the island caves. The Navy had to land on these islands, find and destroy the hideouts, and run the constant risk of ambush.

Clearing a passage through marsh and brambles with cutlasses, David and his men soon had their clothes and shoes cut to pieces by the jagged rocks and thorny cacti. Though it was February, the heat was overpowering and some of the men collapsed; but the rest managed to frighten the pirates into deserting a hideout filled with plunder from English and Spanish vessels. Several caves were found in which a thousand men could hide, and David and his crew set fire to everything after carrying off the loot and ammunition to their vessels. When the men from the ship came to help them, they saluted David, who was acting lieutentant, then burst out laughing, pointing to his clothes. His pantaloons were glued to his legs, his jacket was torn to shreds, and he was covered with mud.

Another time, as they advanced half a mile into the thicket, David heard a great noise to the rear. Thinking the pirates might have "reorganized" to attack behind his force and cut them off, he gave a stirring speech: "Men! Fight bravely! We've dispersed them once. We can do it again, no matter what the odds against us."

Suddenly the men pointed behind him, odd expressions on their faces. "Look, Lieutentant," they roared with laughter. The "attack," David saw, was ten thousand land crabs crunching their way through briars.

Soon the squadron had to return to Key West for supplies, and here his brother, William, whom he had not seen for thirteen years, joined them. David heard the news of home and wished he could visit his sisters in New Orleans. But he was made executive officer of the steamer *Sea Gull*, Commodore Porter's flagship, and was to cruise about the Gulf sounding reefs and shoals.

A dread enemy now struck his ship—yellow fever. Doctors were helpless, not knowing what caused it, how to check it or effect a cure. One after another, the men came down with it— the disease that had killed his mother and Porter's father years before. Twenty-three of the twenty-five officers attacked by the fever died. Commodore Porter became desperately ill, and though he recovered, he was very weak. Their provisions had run out, and David sailed with Porter to Norfolk through forty-three days of rough seas. In Washington, David came down with a slight attack of the fever; but fifteen days later he was visiting friends and "that charming young lady," Susan Marchant, to whom he was now engaged.

After a six weeks' rest at sea, David returned to the West Indies on the *Sea Gull*; and off the Tortugas, near Key West, he asked for a leave to visit his relatives in New Orleans. Sister Nancy, now twenty, did not know him until her foster mother, Mrs. William Boswell, identified him, but they spent a happy ten days together. His father had died and George Antoine, the youngest brother, had been drowned when he was ten. There was no time to visit his sister Elizabeth, a baby when he left home and now adopted by Mrs. DuPont in Pascagoula.

Returning to duty at Key West, he found there was a vacancy on the *Ferret*. By right of seniority David should get the command, but he knew Commodore Porter would not recommend him for fear of showing favoritism. It was only the insistence of Captain Bolton, Captain of the Fleet, that convinced Porter the promotion was rightfully David's.

Farragut was overjoyed. His own command! He went to sea in high spirits searching for pirates off Key West, but they never showed their faces. However, David had to watch closely in navigating his ship through hundreds of tiny reefs or keys dotting those waters. He said, years later, "I have never felt afraid to run a ship since." It was an admirable school for a young officer.

Many cases of fever reappeared on the *Ferret* in a milder form, and David treated these himself—except for one man, who insisted he be put ashore for treatment by a doctor. This doctor had never seen a case of yellow fever and his patient died, but all those treated by David recovered. After a rough voyage to the Bahamas with gales and terrifying thunderstorms, the *Ferret* was ordered home and by the end of July, 1824, David had spent more than a year of hard service in a most unhealthful climate. Once more yellow fever struck him, and for weeks he lay seriously ill in a Washington hospital; but by the last of August he was allowed to visit his friends in Norfolk.

14

Marriage and Promotion

ON SEPTEMBER 2, 1824, David married Susan Marchant and went to Washington to visit the Porters for his honeymoon. These were the last happy weeks the Porter family spent together, for three months later the Commodore's naval career came to an end.

David's physician would not permit him to return to the West Indies, so he was not with Commodore Porter on his expedition to Fajardo, Puerto Rico, in November, 1824. This ended in the court-martial of Porter, his suspension from service for six months, followed by his resignation from the Navy, because he had resented an insult to his flag by a foreigner and had imprisoned him. Porter left the country and spent his self-imposed exile in the Mexican Navy, as American Consul-General to Algiers, and as American Minister to Turkey. Farragut never again saw his foster father, the man who had done more than anyone else to shape his character and fit him for his great naval career.

Financially David was not doing so well for a married man. because for fourteen years he had been a midshipman. He had seen ninety-eight other midshipmen promoted before him, not because they had served longer or were better qualified professionally, but because they were older. All that time he had received only nineteen dollars a month and two rations daily. When he acted as Lieutenant, he got forty dollars a month and three rations each day. Contributing to his sisters' support, he could not save much; nor could he and his wife squander much on a honeymoon. And from August, 1824, until February, 1825, he was not on active duty because yellow fever had left him weakened and his eyes were bothering him.

In August, Farragut's good star finally shone. Commissioned as a lieutenant, he was ordered to the beautiful new frigate *Brandywine*, so named to recall to Lafayette his first battle and his wound. All the officers selected to escort Lafayette home on the *Brandywine* were chosen to represent as many states as possible, and all had to be descendants of those who had fought with distinction in the American Revolution. Lafayette was received aboard with full military honors; the yards were manned and a salute was fired.

In such distinguished company David hoped to hear reminiscences of the General's interesting and romantic career; but once they were at sea, the weather turned so stormy that Lafayette became ill and kept to his cabin.

When he left the ship, Lafayette was asked what he would like as a souvenir; and he requested the flag under which he had been received on board the vessel. David choked up as the flag officer handed it to Lafayette, saying, "Here, General, take it; we could not confide it to more glorious hands."

Back in New York in May, David asked for a half year's leave of absence because his wife was afflicted with neuralgia and his own health was delicate. They went to New Haven for treatment, and during their four months' stay Farragut attended lectures at Yale College. As the result of the sunstroke suffered in Tunis, his eyes were so weak he could not read or write more than a page at a time. So listening to Professor Silliman's chemistry and mineralogy lectures was a real treat.

In October they returned to Norfolk, where Farragut was sent to the receiving ship *Alert*. Since Mrs. Farragut was ailing, Commanding Officer Captain Kennedy arranged for her to live aboard so that David could take better care of her.

At the navy yard Farragut's chief duty was to teach thirty-seven boys, or apprentice seamen, and his worst pupil objected violently to going to school. "I ran away to join the Navy to get out of going to school. I never could l'arn dem letters. It ain't no use."

"Nevertheless," Farragut said to him, "it is my duty to see that you attend classes. If you do not stay here the prescribed time and do your best to learn, I will have to punish you. It will cost you less to study than to loaf."

When the boy remained stubborn, saying, "I'll be blowed if I will l'arn," Farragut took away his liberties. But as time went on he found that with ridicule he accomplished more with the lad. Within a year the reluctant student could write well and became quite expert in mathematics. Farragut was glad to recommend him for the position of yeoman.

Seven years later, on the street one day, a tall young man shook hands heartily with Farragut, who said, "You must mistake me for my brother."

"Oh, no!" retorted the young man. "If I did not know to whom I am more indebted than to anyone else in the world, it would be strange indeed."

"Not my worst pupil aboard the *Alert?*" Farragut asked, surprised.

"The same, and ready to acknowledge you as the greatest benefactor I ever had in this world of trouble"—which made Farragut feel he had not wasted his two years at Norfolk.

For the next ten years he was stationed off and on in Norfolk because of his wife's illness. She had become so helpless that he had to carry her about in his arms like a child. He took her to various cities seeking relief, and all of Norfolk marked the gentle and tender care he gave her. When she died, on December 20, 1840, having been ill the entire sixteen years of their married life, one Norfolk lady said, "When Lieutenant Farragut dies he should have a monument reaching to the skies, made by every wife in the city contributing a stone to it."

In 1832, when South Carolina threatened secession, President Jackson sent Farragut to Charleston with a squadron to bring the followers of John C. Calhoun to terms. He was thus present at the very center of the controversy over nullification during its most dangerous phase.

Next, an assignment in South American waters put him in command of the *Boxer* to Rio. Happy in his second command, Farragut, though he disciplined his men, had a contented and happy crew. When he took his trumpet to give his commands, he saw every man respond cheerfully and intelligently. "I felt like a director leading a symphony orchestra," he said. When his men followed orders perfectly in a difficult maneuver, to the consternation of disapproving crews of English and French men-of-war looking on, he puffed up with pride. His men felt the same about "Little Luff" Farragut, and it was a gratifying six months' cruise.

On August 7, 1838, Farragut got his first rigged ship, the *Erie*, carrying one hundred and forty men. France was then at war with Mexico, demanding payment of damages done to French citizens during the many revolutions in Mexico. The *Erie* was sent to Vera Cruz to protect the rights of American citizens, and Farragut spent much time sounding the reefs and islands thereabouts. He had a chance to study the French fleet under Admiral Baudin, noting the armaments of the ships and the effect of their shots on the forts ashore. The vessels were undamaged by shore fire and only a few men were killed, while the Mexicans suffered the loss of many lives and the fort was almost in ruins.

Invited aboard the French ships, Farragut observed how far in advance they were of American and English vessels. Comparing these newest improvements with his own vessel, fitted as it had been in 1798, Farragut wrote to Commodore Barrow: "If we who wander about the world do not keep those at home informed of daily improvements in other navies, how can we hope to improve, particularly when we see men impressed with the idea that, because they once gained a victory, they can do it again? So they may; but I can tell them it must be with the means of 1838, and not those of 1812." This criticism brought him into disfavor with the Navy Department.

In February, 1841, Farragut was made executive officer of the *Delaware*, a ship of the line of seventy-four guns and twenty-six hundred and thirty-three tons, carrying eight hundred and twenty officers and men. For two months he overhauled her, and for another two months drilled the inexperienced men at the single guns and by divisions until they could fire three aimed broadsides in four minutes—a speed astounding to the gunners of that day.

When finally Farragut gave orders to up the sails, and one after another unfurled to the breeze, he saw his ship like a graceful bird swoop over the waves up the Chesapeake Bay to Annapolis. Standing motionless, he thought, "This is one of the most beautiful things the hands of men have fashioned. And my commands have given it life and motion."

At Annapolis, visitors crowded aboard—as many as two thousand daily. Dignitaries, members of Congress, and foreign visitors came to see the crew go through the exercises with great guns. Two weeks later Farragut was promoted to Commander.

Once more Farragut sailed to Brazil and, after an uneventful six months in those waters, was ordered to the *Decatur*, a sloop of war, returning to Norfolk in February, 1843, after almost two years of pleasant cruising in the South Atlantic.

On December 26, 1843, Farragut was married to Virginia Loyall, member of a prominent Norfolk family. Stationed on the *Pennsylvania*, a receiving ship, at Norfolk, Farragut was glad to be near his bride. When on October 12, 1844, she presented him with a "fine boy whose name is to be Loyall Farragut," he was terribly proud; and the baby's early days were passed on the *Pennsylvania*, where the Farragut family had its living quarters. The proud father fixed a little hammock in which the baby swung above his mother's head during the night, and Farragut had an ingenious arrangement of ropes and pulleys by which he could hoist or lower his son to take care of his needs. His devotion to his boy grew deeper all the years Farragut was stationed at Norfolk, up to the outbreak of war with Mexico.

During this time Farragut dictated all but six pages (written in his own hand) of his autobiography—*Some Reminiscences of Early Life*—using the logbooks from his various cruises and recalling from memory those periods for which the records had been lost.

15

War Clouds Gather

WITH the war in Mexico at hand, Farragut, anxious to see active duty, wrote to the Secretary of the Navy begging for a command—explaining his long service on the Mexican coast; his understanding of the people, their language, and the terrain. But he was refused again and again. Finally in March, 1847, he was given command of the *Saratoga*, which was inadequately manned and supplied. All the way down, he drilled his crew; but when they arrived at Vera Cruz, the castle had capitulated to General Scott's army. Farragut, angry that the Navy had not made the attack, wrote back about some of the naval officers: "Not one of them will ever wear an admiral's flag, which they might have done if that castle had been taken by the Navy." For this criticism he was sent to do blockade duty where he could not possibly distinguish himself.

Ordered to relieve the *Decatur*, his ship was stricken by the yellow fever and, among his crew of one hundred and fifty, ninety-nine cases developed—including Farragut, who had another severe attack which almost ended his life. Yet all this time he had to ride through gales in the blockade off Tuxpan. At last he was asked to come home in February, 1848, when he wrote: "This was the most mortifying of all cruises."

Farragut was delighted to be back at Norfolk with his wife and three-year-old son. But Asiatic cholera laid him low so that, for two more years, ill health kept him in the navy yard doing monotonous routine work. He did arrange exercises for the Ordnance Department of the Navy, with suggestions for improving guns and gunnery; and later he went to Washington to draw up a book of ordnance regulations.

Here he welcomed the chance to attend evening lectures at the Smithsonian Institution. Since his eyes were bad and he could do no reading, he listened eagerly to great men like Elisha Kane, Arctic explorer; President Mark Hopkins of Williams College; Dr. Silliman of Yale; Professor Louis Agassiz of Cambridge.

His brother officers often joked about Farragut's eagerness to learn, and his reply was, "You will rarely come away from such lectures without being somewhat wiser than when you went." He served on courts-martial and, then at Fort Monroe, he superintended experiments designed to test the endurance of different kinds of guns.

When the Crimean War broke out, he thought, "Surely now is my chance to show what I can do." He asked for an assignment abroad, stressing his long interest and service in the Mediterranean and his ability to speak French, Spanish, and Italian. Farragut felt that when sail was giving place to steam, when experiments with ironclad batteries were being made, a seasoned officer like himself should have the chance to study for the Navy the "practical working of the new instruments under tests of war."

Instead, in June, 1854, he was ordered to a post in the opposite direction—to California to establish a new navy yard. This newly acquired territory was rapidly becoming populated after the gold rush of 1849, but to reach it meant a tedious and dangerous journey.

The Farraguts left New York on August 19, 1854, on the *Star of the West*, arriving ten days later in Nicaragua. Here they were transferred to a river steamer and they had to camp on deck with their baggage, protected only by an awning from the heavy dew at night. The crowded conditions on the steamer distressed Farragut, still recovering from his serious illness. So Mrs. Farragut put up a temporary shelter on the deck under the guard rails, protected by an umbrella and shawls, and spent the night fanning him and easing his fever.

But nine-year-old Loyall found the trip exciting. "You should see, Father, the thick jungles and the monkeys and the parrots and—and the men shot some lazy alligators lying in the hot sun."

The next day, instead of the elegant Concord coaches advertised by the transportation companies for California-bound people, canvas-covered wagons met them. These were for the women and children only; the men had to ride horses and mules. Although the road over the mountains was good, the wagons broke down constantly and had to be repaired. At night, in one long room partitioned off with cotton cloth, they slept on deal bunks with canvas bottoms. Then at San Juan del Sur on the Pacific they had to wait several days for the steamer *Cortez* to take them to San Francisco, where they arrived ten days later.

Farragut found San Francisco a boom town and two weeks later took official command of Mare Island, thirty miles away. One unpleasant duty was to get all squatters off the island, an area three miles long and only half a mile wide.

There he was given the *Warren*, a receiving ship, for living quarters, and aboard it they lived for seven months while the commandant's house was being built. Farragut's job was to create a naval yard useful for units of the American Navy stationed in the Pacific—which meant building wharves, docks, sail lofts, carpenter and blacksmith shops, and living quarters for his officers and himself.

Though this was a new kind of work for a seagoing naval officer, Farragut liked it and threw himself into it with his usual energy. He was in full command, with no interference, and he got along well with his workmen. He and Loyall loved watching the boats carrying the workmen back and forth every morning and evening from their homes to the island. He made his men feel they could come to him with their complaints and receive justice; and in return they gave him confidence and loyalty, and enjoyed his generous hospitality. His energy and cordiality increased as his health improved in the stimulating climate. His many years of service in the tropical countries, with attacks of yellow fever and cholera, had made him a partial invalid, but he never gave in to his ills. Now the invigorating air of California, plus his daily horseback rides, restored him to a health he had never known.

In October, 1855, Farragut was delighted to receive word of his promotion to Captain, still the highest rank in the Navy. But his joy was clouded when he learned that his brother, William, was among forty-nine officers recommended by the Retiring Board to be dropped from the Navy without pay. Knowing that William suffered from rheumatism and was unable to carry on in active service, David wrote a stirring protest to the Secretary of the Navy.

He pleaded that William had contracted his disease in the "hardest service I have been engaged in, boat service in the Gulf of Mexico," and had been compelled ever since to "spend more than half his life in bed or on crutches." He maintained that it was a cruel injustice to throw out a penniless officer who had been disabled in the line of duty. The Secretary was moved by the plea, and William was put on a new reserve list for the rest of his life.

Now, deep in the task of building a dock, a marine basin, a railway, and a machine shop during the years 1854 to 1858, Farragut heard little about the gathering clouds of civil war. He knew that the feelings between the North and the South were increasingly bitter, but the fearful tensions east of the Mississippi seemed to cool off after crossing the Rocky Mountains and reaching Mare Island.

Then Mrs. Farragut had to make the long journey home because of the critical illness of her father. Missing her companionship, Farragut leaned more and more on his son, Loyall, with whom he took trips through Calaveras County. During this period many clipper ships rounded the Horn and eventually put into Farragut's new dock. The Russian *Dwina* stopped for repairs and her captain, Butakoff, paid high compliments to Farragut on the efficiency of the facilities afforded him, saluting the *Warren* with thirteen guns on his departure. A French flagship, *Perservante*, under Rear Admiral Lugeol, docked at Mare Island and the Admiral told Farragut, "I'm amazed at the energy these people displayed in so short a time, in constructing a work so essential to the development of the commerce of the Pacific."

Though Farragut completed a complicated project with distinction, it did not make the headlines. But his was an efficient ten-hour-a-day job that, to the Navy Department, showed he was an officer above the ordinary. His complete and detailed reports to the Chief of the Bureau of Yards and Docks, Commander Joseph Smith, greatly impressed and pleased that officer. A few years later, when asked who should be the man to lead the expedition against New Orleans, Smith assured the Secretary of the

Navy, "Farragut! The one above all others for that command."

In August, 1858, Farragut and Loyall sailed for New York, where Mrs. Farragut met them. After several months of visiting at Poughkeepsie, the Farraguts returned to spend Christmas with relatives in Norfolk. There they found the city had been decimated by yellow fever. It was also seething with the fever of political discussion. Farragut was troubled by this whirlpool of political strife, which threatened the very foundations of his beloved country. He was therefore glad to receive his assignment on New Year's Day to the steamer *Brooklyn* at New York. This was a distinct honor, as the *Brooklyn* was one of the five newest and most modern battleships in the Navy. She was a sloop of war, powered by steam, with all her guns mounted on her spar deck.

For Farragut, who had not served on a steamer before, this was a fortunate experience, because this type of vessel was destined in the early days of the Civil War to become the backbone of the fleet with which he won remarkable victories.

A three months' cruise in West Indian and Gulf waters familiarized him with the new craft and enabled him to make suggestions as to changes and improvements throughout the vessel.

Weeks later he had Minister McLane on board bound for Vera Cruz, where they arrived on March the twenty-eighth. Worn out by a number of petty annoyances, including a brush with Navy brass, Farragut was attacked by a fever from which he barely recovered. For several months he conveyed McLane back and forth to his duties, after which he escorted members of a scientific expedition to the Gulf. Among them were Lieutenant Jeffers, the hydrographer, and Captain Frederic Engle, junior to Farragut in command.

Later he learned that Engle, for whom he always had friendly feelings, had written to the Secretary of the Navy: "It gives me pleasure to say that Captain Farragut has afforded me every facility for fulfilling my duty with energy and dispatch. He is an able and accomplished seaman, and runs his ship with the ability and confidence of one."

On his return to Norfolk, Farragut shared the gloom and anxiety over the widening breach between the North and the South. On December 20, 1860, South Carolina seceded from the Union; and by February, Mississippi, Florida, Alabama, Georgia, Louisiana, and Texas had followed. Delegates from these states met at Montgomery, Alabama, to set up a new government—The Confederate States of America. Then, under Virginia's leadership, a Peace Convention assembled at Washington to attempt conciliation, but to no avail.

Registered in the Navy as a native of Tennessee, Farragut had made his home in Norfolk for years and looked upon Virginia as his adopted state. Both his wives were born in Virginia, and the present Mrs. Farragut had four sisters and brothers, with many other relatives, all living in Virginia. So they all hoped and prayed that civil war might be avoided.

Virginians had helped in winning United States independence, in framing the Constitution; and five Virginians had been Presidents of the United States. Though Lincoln's election had been a disappointment to many in Norfolk, a large number of its citizens were opposed to secession. When delegates were chosen for the convention to decide whether Virginia was to secede, the Unionist delegate was elected by a majority of two to one.

Throughout all the mad discussions Farragut steadfastly opposed secession. He had been at Charleston while General Scott was carrying out President Jackson's mandate to preserve the Union then threatened by the nullifiers. He had observed the results of civil wars in the Argentine, Brazil, Uruguay, Mexico;

and when he met naval officers and citizens at a local store to discuss the daily events, he pointed out the horrors of civil war. For this he was called a "croaker" and ridiculed.

When President Lincoln in his inaugural speech declared he would use force to maintain the Union, demands for Virginia's immediate secession poured in from all over the state. Farragut was in the crowd gathered in Mechanics Hall, in Norfolk, where fiery addresses demanded that their delegate vote for secession, though he had been elected as a Union conservative. Farragut left the hall late that night, tired and sick at heart.

Then came Lincoln's attempt to reinforce Fort Sumter, the firing on the fort, and its capture by Southern troops. On the following Sunday at church, Farragut heard that the prayer for the President of the United States was to be omitted from the service. If so, Farragut decided to walk out; but the service was read as usual. When the psalm for the day began, "Samaria is desolate," Farragut remarked to his wife, "There's prophecy for you! God help the country!"

Two days later, on April the fifteenth, came Lincoln's call for seventy-five thousand volunteers, and the convention in a wild hysterical scene voted for secession eighty-five to fifty-five. For days, business had practically stopped in Norfolk; and now the militia paraded the streets with music and Southern flags.

To a gathering at the store next morning Farragut remarked, "Virginia has been dragooned out of the Union." Abruptly he sensed the hostility in his brother officers' attitude toward him. He learned that most of the Southern naval officers had already sent in their resignations, though some had done so with great regret.

He tried to argue with them. "Mr. Lincoln," he insisted, "has every right to call out troops to defend government property. In fact, it is his duty."

Coldly an officer replied, "Virginia has seceded, Captain Farragut. Either you resign from the United States Navy or you leave Norfolk."

Could these be the men who had been his friends for years— these men whose faces were tight with anger? "Very well," Farragut sadly replied. "Naturally I cannot live here any longer, so I'll find a place where a Union man can live. And I'll do it on two hours' notice." No one said good-bye as he turned his back on the group and left.

Returning home, extremely downcast, he was scarcely conscious of the spring flowers just bursting into bloom in the lovely Virginia gardens he passed. In deep distress he wondered how he could explain to his wife what had happened in the store. But he entered the house resolutely to tell her he had decided to stand by the Union flag.

"I know all your friends and relatives are here, my dear," he said. "But to me this question is far bigger than they. This act of mine may cause years of separation from them; so you must decide quickly whether you will go North with me or remain here. There may be fighting in Norfolk and I don't want to be ordered to raise my hand against our friends and neighbors. I must leave this very day."

Though it had been hard for him, he was asking her to make a much more difficult decision. She would have to break off from people she had known all her life, as well as from her nearest and dearest relatives. Yet her devotion and courage were equal to his, for promptly she said, "I shall go where you go."

Hurriedly she collected a few of their most prized possessions, and they went to Grandfather Loyall's home to say their sad farewells. Then Mrs. Farragut; her sister, Mrs. Ashe, with her two small children; and an old family Negro servant-woman, Sinah— these five climbed into a carriage and rode to the wharf.

Farragut and his son, Loyall, now sixteen years old, chose to walk side by side through the town. They heard muttered curses and saw scowling faces along the way. Someone snarled, "Traitor!" Fists were shaken at them as they passed and, expecting more heckling, Farragut placed his hand comfortingly on his son's shoulder.

As if sensing his father's concern, Loyall whispered, "Will they try to arrest you, Father? They are very angry."

"No, I think not. They know that a man must do what he thinks is right. They have a right to act on their own conscience, as I do."

"But you are right, Father," Loyall insisted as he adjusted his step to his father's.

Farragut wondered, "Is there any right in an act that sets brother against brother?" A few days before, every man in Norfolk had been his friend; now most of them were his enemies.

He did not know that some who watched him leave wondered if they would ever see him again, for at this time Farragut was almost sixty years old and beginning to show his age. His black hair was graying and thinning out, a fact which he concealed by combing a lock over the bald spot. He weighed a bare one hundred and fifty pounds, not too much for his height of five feet six inches. Tanned and weather-beaten by continual exposure, his face was deeply lined and his swarthy skin looked like leather. He had prominent features: his ears, nose, and mouth were large; and his eyes, because of their weakness, gave a quizzical half-smiling appearance to his face.

He thought, "They must see me as a man whose public life is over, whose service has been one of dull routine with little chance of promotion or professional distinction." His mildness of manner and speech gave no hint of the rugged courage and fearless determination that would mark his remarkable naval victories in the next few years.

The Farraguts arrived in Baltimore in the early afternoon of April 19, finding the city noisy and bustling with preparations for war. A short time before, a mob had fired on a Massachusetts regiment marching south to defend Washington. Railroad bridges over the Susquehanna River had been destroyed, forcing the exiles to travel by canal boat, crowded with three hundred passengers, to Philadelphia. From there to New York the journey was more comfortable.

After placing Mrs. Ashe and her children on a steamer for California, Farragut took his family to Hastings-on-Hudson, where he rented a cottage. Awaiting orders among people who held all Southeners under hatred and suspicion might not be easy, Farragut knew.

16

Capture of the Queen of the Gulf

FROM April to December, Farragut watched the Federal authorities go muddling and blundering from Bull Run into a series of military disasters—while he waited for his orders to active duty, growing more impatient each day. He and his family made some pleasant new acquaintances who were very friendly, but he hated these months of idleness so far from the scenes of battle. Because he was restless he took long walks daily over the surrounding beautiful hills, and immediately the villagers' tongues began to wag.

"Yes, his long rambles are only a cloak for perfecting plans for destroying the Croton Aqueduct in order to cut off the water supply to New York City."

"That must be so! Doesn't the aqueduct run only thirty feet in back of the Farragut cottage?"

They would have been convinced he was a Southern spy if they had known that he was visiting shipyards in the vicinity of New York where naval vessels were being constructed. He saw the keel of the Monitor laid but, not liking ironclads, was not impressed.

His first orders were to Brooklyn Navy Yard, where he sat, "day after day, turning the pages of the Navy Register and listening to the chatter of old commodores and medicos, about dropping some poor devil from the service."

But the Navy Department was moving cautiously, "careful and guarded whom to trust, and in the employment of Southern officers particularly circumspect," said Secretary of the Navy Gideon Welles.

What Farragut did not know was that his name came up again and again as the Navy Department in Washington planned a grand strategy to open the Mississippi River. If the Union could get the Mississippi in its hands it could cut a path through the Confederacy, separating the Western States from the Eastern. Then the many navigable rivers running into the Mississippi would be highways on which the Union gunboats could execute raids into the very heart of the country east and west.

Then, too, the Queen of the Gulf, New Orleans, situated near the mouth of the river, was the largest city in the South, an exporting center of tremendous importance. Cotton was the foundation of the Confederacy—since she had practically a world monopoly on that staple, and cotton was exchanged for all her war materials from England and France. New Orleans, the trade center of this industry, was the soft underside and vulnerable part of the Southern Confederacy.

Soon after the war broke out, a flotilla of hurriedly patched-together gunboats was put on the Mississippi to fight a way south from the mouth of the Ohio. Now if a squadron of heavy ships could work from the Gulf, the Mississippi River would be in

Union hands when the two met. Though chiefly a Navy plan, cooperation from the Army was needed to guarantee success.

Therefore the command for New Orleans had to be, said Secretary Welles, "under a leader who had courage, audacity, tact and fearless energy, with great self-reliance, decisive judgement and ability to discriminate and act under trying and extraordinary circumstances."

The seamen, hearing that their commander, Commodore McKean, was ill and another had to be appointed for the Gulf Squadron, immediately said, "Pick Captain Davy Farragut to take his place. If Davy came down here, it wouldn't be long till the fur was flying."

Commander Joseph Smith, remembering Farragut's efficiency at Mare Island, spoke up. "Farragut! Above all others for that command!" Assistant Secretary of the Navy, Fox, recalled how quickly Farragut left Norfolk and came North to offer his services. Secretary Welles then remembered Farragut's daring plan to take the castle near Vera Cruz in 1838, and time had proved him right. Then David D. Porter, the second son of Farragut's foster father, expressed his confidence, so he was sent to ask Farragut if he would like the job.

Would he? This was a chance beyond his fondest dreams! Two days before Christmas, in 1861, Farragut was called to Washington, excited as a small boy with a Christmas toy he had always wanted. After the New Year he received his orders for his squadron, of which the *Hartford* was to be his flagship. Farragut and his officers and men became greatly attached to her, and even Mrs. Farragut called her "dear old *Hartford*."

This ship was to be associated with his name as the *Victory* is with Lord Nelson's, for next to the *Constitution* the *Hartford* became the most famous vessel in the Navy as a winner of victories. Like the *Brooklyn*, it was the most modern type of man-of-war in the American fleet.

By February, Farragut had completed his plans for sailing his *Hartford* to the Gulf and began preparations for the attack. His orders were to gather as many vessels as could be spared from the blockade and proceed up the Mississippi. He would reduce the defense of New Orleans, take possession of it under guns of his squadron, and hold it until troops came.

Farragut made Pensacola his base in the rear, and Ship Island his rendezvous point of action. This island lies about one hundred miles north of the passes of the Mississippi and directly off the entrance to Lake Pontchartrain, where Farragut used to go sailing on his father's yawl fifty years before. Here he laid his plans and assembled the ships. As flag officer, Farragut would be in command of a fleet that was one of the largest ever assembled by the American Navy.

As usual his first thought was for the comforts of his men and, knowing many would be hurt, he wanted proper equipment for the sick and the wounded. Remembering the French at Vera Cruz, he asked that a frigate be outfitted as a hospital ship with facilities for getting his wounded aboard without torment. So began his plea for more medical officers and more hospital supplies, which he would be begging for throughout his service in the Gulf.

Since the Confederates had an excellent spy system, they knew what was in the wind as soon as the *Hartford* arrived at Ship Island. Immediately they strengthened their defense at the passes and forts to make New Orleans impregnable.

As each ship joined him, Farragut boarded it to check carefully all preparations for the attack—to make sure everything would be in readiness when the hour to strike came. He wanted each officer to know his part in the plan, and he briefed them all repeatedly. He impressed upon each seamen, "You must be prepared to execute all those duties to which you have been so long trained in the Navy." Each sailor stood more erect, his face stern, knowing that his commander depended on him.

When everything was ready and Porter arrived with his mortar fleet, Farragut would dash up the river; but he did not want the enemy to learn of his plan before he was ready. He wanted them to think Mobile would be the first object of attack, and chafed at the delay in the arrival of eighteen thousand troops and the six warships ordered to join him. Welles had written that Farragut was to open the way to the sea for the West.

But before he could attack, he had to conquer mud. The mouths of the Mississippi spread like a scrawny chicken's foot out into the Gulf of Mexico, and these five mouths, or passes, each had a bar of sediment left there by Old Man River. Since these deposits were continually shifting, pilots had to sound channels constantly and dredge to keep them free of the mucky obstruction. Thus Farragut's first worry was to get his heavier ships across the bars.

Above these passes where the river made its first big bend were the chief military defenses of New Orleans—Fort St. Philip on the north bank and Fort Jackson on the south. If Farragut managed to get by these defenses, the Confederates had built a shore battery beyond and had collected a flotilla of fifteen small vessels —among them a new ironclad, *Merrimac*.

Below Fort Jackson heavy chains had been stretched across the river, connected with a boom of huge cypress logs moored with seven anchors. Though spring floods broke this, a stronger barrier was built with ten chains supported by eight hulks anchored across the river.

So Farragut's job at the mouth of the Mississippi was like nothing he had ever faced before. He must raise his vessels over the mud bars by tediously lightening each ship and then towing it with tugboats against the strong current. When all his large units were taken care of, he had to break a passage in the barrier wide enough to steam through. And there was still the defense flotilla stationed above, ready to pour a raking fire upon Union boats as they headed upstream. The danger of running aground and being left helpless under fire from batteries, gunboats, and sharpshooters hidden on the banks would be ever present. But first the *Colorado*, the *Pensacola*, and the *Mississippi*—all had to be sent back to Ship Island to be lightened.

To get his fleet into the river, for his heavy ships Farragut chose the Southwest Pass; the mortar schooners were to go through the opposite end—the Passe à l'Outré. One by one he succeeded in dragging his heaviest vessels over the bar—all except the largest, the frigate *Colorado*. About this he wrote his wife: "Success is the only thing listened to in this war, and I know I must sink or swim by this rule. Two of my best friends have done me great injury by telling the Department that the *Colorado* can be gotten over the bar . . . and so I was compelled to try it, and take precious time to do it. If I had been left to myself, I would have been in before this."

The *Colorado* finally had to furnish extra guns and men to the other ships. The *Pensacola* and the *Mississippi*, stripped of everything but coal enough to steam with, were pulled through a foot of mud by tugs.

Farragut remained confident, for he knew what he was up against and he did not mind the hard work. If only the people back home and in the Navy Department would not demand victory before he was ready to attempt it!

To his wife he wrote: "I have now attained what I have been looking for all my life—a flag—now all that is necessary to complete the scene is a victory. If I die in the attempt, it will only be what every officer has to expect. He who dies in doing his duty to his country, and at peace with his God, has played out the drama of life to the best advantage."

It had taken ten days of pulling and hauling to get the *Mississippi* over, and two weeks more for the *Pensacola* to move into the river. If only the coal, men, ships, and supplies he had demanded would come! But so far he had no word that the Navy had even heard of his needs.

By April he wrote his wife: "The defeat of our army at Corinth . . . will give us a much harder fight; men are easily elated or depressed by victory. *But as to being prepared for defeat, I certainly am not. Any man who is prepared for defeat would be half defeated before he commenced.* I hope for success, shall do all in my power to receive it and trust to God for the rest. I trust in Him as a merciful being; but really in war it seems as if we hardly ought to expect mercy when men are destroying one another upon questions of which He alone is judge."

At the head of the passes Farragut now had seventeen men-of-war and Porter's mortar flotilla, twenty in number. Now he checked all ships carefully to protect the crews and vessels from all hazards. Sheet cables were arranged on the sides of ships to form a kind of chain armor for the engines. Bags of sand were stacked about the engines and machinery, down in the storerooms along the water line, in the hold to protect the surgeons, in the bows, under the topgallant forecastle to stop raking shots, around the guns, and against the bulwarks. Large nettings of two-inch ropes were arranged to cover the decks and protect the men from falling spars and splinters. Ships, including guns and rigging, were daubed with mud to make them invisible at night. Decks and gun carriages were whitewashed so that handspikes, tackle falls, and ammunition could be more readily seen during attacks in darkness. Grapnels and chains were put into whaleboats for towing fire rafts away from the vessels.

From early dawn to dark, Farragut was everywhere in the fleet —often at six in the morning hailing the watch officer to ask if all was well. He liked to see the men spring to answer his command with determination and confidence. He joked with them in friendly talk, which they returned with the prompt carrying out of his orders and with worship in their eyes. In the days that followed, Farragut slept in snatches—little cat naps—sitting upright in his chair, completely exhausted.

Months before, Porter had promised the Navy Department that his bomb vessels could reduce Fort Jackson and Fort St. Philip in forty-eight hours. Farragut, doubting it but willing to let Porter try it, gave him permission on April the eighteenth to do so. However, to make it harder for the fort gunners to locate these mortar schooners, Farragut ordered a young tree lashed to each mast. The trick worked, for not one of these bomb vessels was spotted by the Confederate gunners.

For six days and nights Porter's mortars blasted away. The Confederates set fire to rafts piled high with wood smeared with tar and turpentine, and Farragut had to send boats to grapple and tow the burning barges out of his way. Then at two in the morning of the twenty-fourth of April, 1862, two red lights at the peak of his flagship gave the signal for the fleet to get under way. Two officers with a squad of men rowed up to the barrier and, under fire, disconnected the chains and logs to make an opening wide enough for the ships to pass through. Farragut walked the deck all night in his anxiety, until an officer reported, "The darkness helped, sir. The job is done. Not a man was hurt."

Captain Theodorus Bailey, leading one column, was to dash past Fort St. Philip while Farragut, at the head of the other column, would pass Fort Jackson. Many of the officers felt that the ships could not pass the forts, and Farragut heard his surgeon say of him, "He may be a bold, brave officer, but does he *know* what he is about?" Against their opinions he decided to by-pass the forts before they had been reduced.

Bursting shells from the forts crisscrossed the heavens like comets with tails of fire, and the men were ordered to lie down until their own guns could be brought into range. In the preceding six days of shelling by Porter's mortars, the fort guns had been only slightly damaged.

Suddenly, bearing down swiftly on the *Hartford*, came a blazing mass—a fire raft pushed by a tug. The river was narrow here and the *Hartford*, nosing into the mud to avoid the raft, stuck. Now the tug pushed the raging inferno against the port quarter of the ship, and tongues of fire started to lick up the mizzen rigging. Farragut's signal officer, Osborn, rolled three twenty-pound shells across the deck and, under heat so great that he had to cover his head with his coat, he uncapped them. Then he rolled the shells over the side onto the burning raft, and instantly a terrific roar and blazing light revealed a big hole in her. Springing up with hoses, the fire crew drenched the flames aboard the *Hartford* while boat crews grappled the raft to tow it away. Guns opened up on the tug, which ran for cover while the flagship's engines backed hard. Finally the *Hartford* eased off the mud into deep water and continued upstream, Farragut mopping perspiration off his face as he thought how his attack had been near failing before it had scarcely begun!

With her crew lying flat on deck, the *Richmond* followed; and as they came abreast of Fort Jackson the gunners jumped to their feet, opening fire with grape and canister at a stone's-throw range of the fort. The ship throbbed with the beat of her engines, and trembled with the shocks from the firing of her big guns. A captain of a gun crew was decapitated and, as his body fell, the lockstring in his hand was pulled and the gun discharged.

Crossing the river, the *Richmond* gave Fort St. Philip a few parting broadsides; and then she, too, was above the forts. The land batteries were blazing away with all they had, but in the darkness and smoke it was not easy to get the range of the invading fleet or to aim at any definite object. The defenders were unable to do serious damage to a single one of the approaching ships.

Bailey's gunboats all got through the barrier and past the forts, and all but three of Fleet Captain Henry Bell's division. These retired downstream to await further orders.

Above the forts the enemy forces were so thick that what missed one rebel hit another, and their light gunboats were a poor match for Farragut's heavy sloops of war. But one Confederate vessel, the *Governor Moore*, put the Union gunboat *Varuna* out of action by a dashing attack at close quarters—forcing her to make for shore, where she sank in the reeds.

The *Mississippi*, under Lieutenant George Dewey, was rammed by the *Manassas*, which had also strafed seven other Union ships but without doing serious damage. Finally the *Mississippi* rushed at her full speed, crowding her ashore, then turned and poured broadsides into her. The enemy crew escaped into the swamp, while the *Manassas* slid off the bank, floated downstream, and sank.

On the way up, the Union *Cayuga* discovered a regiment camped on shore; and Lieutenant Perkins shouted to the officers to come aboard and surrender. Down came the colors, and Colonel Symanski delivered over his sword—seven hundred troops on land surrendering to a single gunboat!

In Farragut's fleet the casualties were thirty-seven killed and one hundred and forty-nine wounded, and during the preceding six-day bombardment the losses had been two killed and thirty wounded. Though his own flagship had been struck eighteen times and two guns disabled, and all the other vessels damaged in some degree, no shots had hit dangerously near the water line.

The Confederate casualties in the forts were eleven killed and thirty-seven wounded, and on their ships seventy-three killed and seventy-three wounded. Eight Confederate craft had been destroyed, and only two of their river gunboats escaped up the river.

Gratified that his fleet had come through with so small a loss of life, Farragut ordered that, at eleven o'clock on the twenty-sixth, all officers and crews should return "thanks to Almighty God for his great goodness and mercy in permitting us to pass through the events of the last two days with so little loss of life and blood."

As his fleet steamed up the river to New Orleans, Farragut saw twenty ships, laden with cotton and set afire, floating down the river. Overhead was a reflected red glare in the sky from the burning of thirteen thousand bales of cotton which had been dumped into the water to prevent them from falling into Union hands. "What a terrible waste!" he thought. He remembered his first glimpse of New Orleans fifty-four years before, at the end of the long keelboat voyage from Tennessee. Now, on his day of victory, his brother William's children were living in this conquered city and near by, at Pascagoula, dwelt his two sisters and their families. How would they feel toward him, coming at the head of a great Northern fleet about to take possession of their city?

At one o'clock the Hartford came to anchor, and the others soon after. Rain was pouring down in torrents accompanied by thunder and lightning, but it could not quench the smoldering fires consuming the great piles of abandoned cotton, coal, ships, and docks. Instead, it caused billowing clouds of black smoke to hang low over the river and city. Now, floating downstream, all ablaze, came the unfinished Confederate ram Mississippi, a sad sight and a grim omen to the watching crowds on shore.

At three o'clock Captain Bailey and Lieutenant Perkins went ashore to demand that the flag be hauled down; and a mob followed them to the City Hall, hooting and shouting. Some carried weapons and yelled "Hang them! Hang them!" but two respected local citizens escorted the officers safely to the mayor's office.

The mayor protested that New Orleans was under martial law and they would have to wait for General Lovell, who was in command. The next day Captain Bell led a body of marines ashore, where he and two of his men hauled the Confederate colors down and hoisted the Stars and Stripes over the City Hall, the Custom House, and the Post Office. The city had the meager satisfaction of knowing she had not lowered her colors with her own hands. Porter was sent to demand the surrender of the forts, and soon afterward General Butler landed his troops and occupied New Orleans. The Queen of the Gulf had been captured.

Farragut went to his cabin to write a letter: "My Dearest Wife and Boy: I am so agitated that I can scarcely write, and shall only tell you it has pleased Almighty God to preserve my life through such a fire as the world has scarcely known."

That was literally true, for he had been standing throughout the entire running fight in the most exposed position on the deck of the *Hartford*. He seemed to be breathing flames. Men had been struck down around him, yet he had escaped untouched.

Up North it was some time before they realized what Farragut had done, but the South knew immediately that his successful campaign meant not only the loss of a great city but also the loss of the war. Napoleon's failure to recognize the Confederacy was due to Farragut's capture of New Orleans; and if he had failed, a few months later after McClellan's crushing defeat in Virginia, England would have taken steps toward bringing about peace, with the establishment of the Confederate States of America as an independent nation!

Thus Farragut's capture of the Queen of the Gulf was a turning point in the course of the Civil War, and the Union might yet be saved. Nearly fifty years before, in Tunis, Consul Folsom had given Midshipman Farragut a Turkish yataghan (sword), and the scabbard had an embossed scene showing a frigate passing between the fire of two forts. It presented a strange prophecy of what Farragut succeeded in doing at New Orleans.

Yet, in the glow of victory, Farragut felt sad about the antagonism shown toward him in the city. One day when he and his fleet surgeon, Jonathan Foltz, entered a streetcar, Farragut sat near a well-dressed woman and her small daughter. The little girl stroked the gold braid on his uniform and said, "Look, Mamma! Pretty!"

Fond of children, Farragut smilingly patted her head, saying, "You are a dear little girl."

Suddenly the mother turned and spat in Farragut's face and jerked her child away. "You murderer!" she screamed. "You'd kill even the women and children."

Foltz grabbed her wrists and reproached her, but Farragut touched his arm and said calmly, "Remember that this city is under the guns of my fleet. Many lives may be sacrificed and the city destroyed because of this foolish woman. She can easily provoke a riot."

Meanwhile he wiped his face, and the woman, hearing "guns of my fleet," quieted down. She shook her head at the people who had come up to ask, "What's happened?"

Thinking of his own brother William's family and his two sisters, none of whom had come to see him, Farragut wrote to his wife: "Strange! I am here among relatives and yet no one has dared to say, 'I am happy to see you.'" It was a heavy personal price to pay in his hour of victory over the Queen of the Gulf.

17

First Rear Admiral — David Farragut

I N the next few weeks Farragut found himself in the newspaper headlines everywhere as the "Hero of New Orleans." He joked about that in his letters to his wife, writing: "But I must keep moving and keep up this stampede." On to Mobile was his plan; for after New Orleans fell, Mobile Bay became a very valuable outlet for Southern cotton as well as an inlet for British munitions. And as he would not need heavy, slow land forces to support him, he could strike now.

But the Navy had its own plans for opening the whole Mississippi and, because he had captured New Orleans in one brilliant stroke, it was decided he could take Vicksburg the same way. First he was ordered to take Natchez and Baton Rouge, which surrendered quickly late in June of 1862. But Vicksburg defied him, and he knew he needed the army to cut off communications by land; without land action he saw no chance of forcing surrender on the Gibraltar of the West.

The river campaigning was hard on his ships and men, for both were under constant fire from the forts and batteries and from hidden bands of snipers. Trying to navigate in the channel, the large vessels often collided; and submerged snags and shifting bars caused trouble. Under the strain of river navigation, the engines broke down again and again. "Dilapidated vessels trying to go a thousand miles against a strong current," Farragut wrote to Bailey.

Another great trouble was illness; many of his men were suffering from fever, dysentery, and diarrhea. Then the river fell and his boats got stuck on mud banks, "five hundred miles from the natural element of a sailor."

Despite all obstacles, on June the twenty-eighth Farragut ordered a start at dawn—following with Porter the same procedure they had used at New Orleans—and within three hours his fleet had successfully passed the batteries of Vicksburg. The move brought him closer to Flag Officer Davis' river flotilla, working down from the North—which meant the whole Mississippi would be patrolled by Union vessels.

But Vicksburg lay behind and must be reduced before the entire river could be in Union control. Writing to his wife, Farragut said: "It seems as if the fleet is to simmer between these steep banks. Insects smite us from every side. Fever, chills and dysentery, and just plain *nothing to do* will defeat us. We'll lose all the fleet has won in honor and reputation. Must we spend the rest of the year in this hottest of holes?"

By the middle of July he was enduring more annoyance and suffering more mental anguish. His fleet had gone to the mouth of the Yazoo River—where the enemy had just built a new iron-clad ram, the *Arkansas*. On July the fourteenth, clouds of smoke belching from their funnels, the Union gunboats *Tyler* and *Queen of the West* fled toward the fleet, chased by the *Arkansas*.

In defiance of the entire Union fleet the *Arkansas* came on, rounding the point at full speed. Farragut's vessels could not get up steam quickly enough to maneuver, because their fires were banked; and so closely packed were they in their formation that they dared not fire for fear of hitting one another. All they could do was take the running fire of the *Arkansas* as she went booming along through the whole Union fleet to escape and take cover under the Vicksburg batteries.

Farragut knew the Confederates exulted in this daring spectacle but realized it was just that, accomplishing nothing; to him it was truly mortifying. Though his fleet finally went in search of the rebel *Arkansas*, they could see "nothing but the flash of the enemy guns to fire at." And the attempt cost the fleet eighteen killed, fifty wounded, and ten missing.

"The ram must be attacked and destroyed," said Bell to him, "or, sir, she will destroy us." But after eight maddening days of continual failure to force the *Arkansas* out of hiding, Farragut received orders to "go down river at your discretion." The men, prostrated by sickness and the terrible heat, found it even a "terrible fatigue to coal ship" and were glad to retire down the river in two columns.

Confederate General Van Dorn, at Vicksburg, telegraphed President Davis: "The whole of the lower Union fleet and all the troops have disappeared down the river." For Farragut, July of 1862 was the lowest ebb during the war.

But Commander William D. Porter—the very one who had been the tiny baby whom Farragut saw when he came to live with the Porters in New Orleans fifty years before—was determined to finish off the *Arkansas*, and made a gallant attack on her as she lay under the Vicksburg batteries—only to run aground and fail.

A few days later, catching her out in the river, he shelled her so furiously that she was disabled and abandoned by her crew. The *Arkansas* was fired, her moorings were cut, and she was set adrift down the river—and when the flames reached her magazines her brief career was ended in a fearful explosion.

To Farragut this campaign seemed long and costly, but the feeling of admiration for him—from official Washington down to the plain people—grew. By August his promotion to the new rank of Rear Admiral came, with an official letter of thanks to his officers and men. Hoisting the new Admiral's flag at the main, he called all hands on his flagship and read them the letter to the loud cheers of the ship's company. Then he sent it to be read on every vessel of the fleet.

Now he was free to return to his base at Pensacola for personal rest, and for the long-needed refitting and repairs of his ships. At the same time he maintained a close blockade of the Gulf coast and the mouths of the Mississippi. At Pensacola his son, Loyall, joined him for a visit, proud of his father's achievements.

Here Farragut asked for smaller boats fast enough to catch the blockade runners, many of which eluded him. By November the health of his crew had been restored; his ships were in better repair, and the blockade was operating more efficiently.

While Farragut was refitting his Gulf Squadron at Pensacola, the Confederates strengthened their defenses at all strategic points. One stronghold was a serious threat to the Union control of the river—Port Hudson, lying just south of the opening of the highly important Red River. It, too, was on a hairpin bend of the Mississippi, making it a dangerous place for maneuvering seagoing vessels. A perilous shoal lay in the middle of the river, forcing ships to hug the shore on which the Confederates had erected strong batteries. The bluff was only fifty feet high; but the current sweeping below swirled in eddies and treacherous pools, confusing to a navigating officer.

Port Hudson presented a new tactical problem. An army of twelve thousand men was to assemble at Baton Rouge and march on the fort while Farragut attacked from the river. Since many units of his original fleet had been sent farther north for repairs, he had only four large ships, three gunboats, and the flotilla of mortar schooners protected by two more gunboats. He directed his first three ships to advance, each with a gunboat lashed to the side away from the forts. His idea was that if—in running so necessarily close to Confederate guns—a ship should be disabled, the undamaged gunboat could tow her on into safe water.

He ordered his ships to draw more forward than aft, so that if a vessel was grounded she would not be swung around by the current but held upstream on her bow. Sandbags were packed around vulnerable parts of the ships, such as the engine rooms, and once again Farragut would attempt a night attack. But the *Mississippi*, an ungainly side-wheeler with huge paddle boxes, could not lash on a gunboat.

In a letter to his captains he wrote memorable words, treasured among naval men as the whole art of battle expressed in one sentence: *"I think the best protection against the enemy's fire is a well-directed fire from our own guns."*

At dark on March 14, 1863, the *Hartford's* signal lantern gleamed red, and the ships filed into position with Farragut leading. His son, Loyall, was on the poop deck near him, and Fleet Surgeon Foltz suggested, "Admiral, it would be safer to have Loyall down with me on the berth deck. It's more protected there, sir."

"Oh, no, Father! I want to be on deck to see the fight," cried Loyall indignantly.

Farragut understood how Loyall felt but knew he would worry about his son's exposure to danger, especially when he needed a clear mind as Commander of the Fleet.

"He could help me with the wounded," urged Surgeon Foltz.

"No. True, he's not in service and only by chance is he aboard," said Farragut. "But he will act as my aide, conveying orders during battle, and we will trust in Providence."

The Confederate pickets spied the Union fleet and signaled their batteries by sending up rockets. Immediately a roar of cannon followed, and Farragut's mortar boomed; then, as the *Hartford's* guns bore, they also began firing. Confederate locomotive headlights were turned on the river, and then the enemy set fire to huge piles of lightwood on the westerly bank. This threw a glare over the water by which the shore gunners were able to aim almost as well as if it were day.

The *Hartford* stood out in the firelight as clear as a silhouette, but a moment later, when she fired her broadside guns, clouds of smoke enveloped her and she was lost to sight. As other ships opened fire on the shore batteries, the smoke spread over the water, swelled up, fogged in the fleet until nothing was seen from the shore but a flame-riven cloud drifting slowly upstream.

Blinded by the smoke, the *Hartford* pilot, Thomas R. Carroll, standing in the mizzen, called through the tube, "I can no longer guide the ship aright."

Farragut ordered, "Silence the guns!" As the smoke rolled away, he saw the current was driving her on the eastern shore. With the bluffs so close, he could hear the Confederates call to one another; and in a moment the jar told him she had grounded.

But now his strategy paid off. The gunboat *Albatross*, lashed to the side of the *Hartford*, reversed her engines full speed at the same time the *Hartford* did, enabling Farragut to clear the bank and round the point. Meanwhile the *Richmond*, following him and unable to see, came so close that she put her bowsprit almost over the *Hartford's* stern.

To avoid any further collisions, Farragut decided to steam ahead, out of the way, at full speed. He had already been under continuous fire for an hour, and would have to run past batteries which extended for a mile and a quarter along the river. Abreast of these the river was so strong that the *Hartford* crawled at a man's walking pace.

Clouds of powder smoke rolled down over Farragut as they passed up the river, and shot fell all around. But when the forts were passed and he turned to look for the other ships of his fleet, he exclaimed, "My God, what happened to the others!"

Amid the battle smoke a flickering streak of red flame shot up, and from his masthead came the cry, "A ship's afire! Looks like the *Mississippi*."

During a brief lull in ship and shore firing, the Admiral saw clearly that his other ships had not made the turn and were still below Port Hudson. As the cannonading slackened, the *Mississippi* stood outlined in flames; fire was licking up the tarred rigging, setting the upper masts ablaze. Then the loaded guns, heated by the fire, exploded with a deafening roar. Now, her entire lower rigging ablaze, she drifted with the current; and when the fire reached her magazines, she suddenly blew up with a terrific explosion.

Later Farragut learned that the *Mississippi*, while driving past the batteries, had run ashore so hard that she could not free herself, even though the *Essex* steamed up to help her. After thirty-five minutes of splashing paddle wheels, and helpless against Confederate shot hurled into her hull, Captain Smith ordered her abandoned. His executive officer, Lieutenant George Dewey, stayed with him to the end, rescuing wounded and others of her crew.

With his largest ship destroyed, Farragut found himself alone with only the *Albatross* above Port Hudson. Though the *Hartford* had been under the fire of the batteries, taking considerable beating in hull and rigging, her machinery was intact. One man had been killed and two were slightly wounded.

Farragut learned later that his other vessels had suffered so much in their attempt to run the forts that they had to give up, and General Banks, who was to have cut off Port Hudson in the rear, was stopped before he got anywhere. The whole plan was a failure in Farragut's eyes, and in his report to Secretary Welles he took full responsibility.

Though Farragut was proud of the way his son, Loyall, had taken his baptism of fire—as "a Farragut should"—he sent him home, writing to his wife: "The anxieties of a father should not be added to those of a commander."

Now the Admiral planned to make the best of a plan gone wrong. His ship, with the *Albatross*, could steam up the river to block the point where the Red River emptied into the Mississippi. This was an important artery for the Confederacy, bringing from the West food and grain needed for the armies in the East. Harassed by sniping from shore, Farragut still was able to destroy several small vessels loaded with supplies for the Confederates; and he dropped anchor a few miles below Vicksburg, where he was able to replenish with coal from Grant. Then he joined in the siege of Port Hudson—Port Gibson today—where earlier he had cut telegraph communications.

Tedious, hot summer weeks followed, during which Farragut kept a blockade of the Red River and strengthened communications between the lower and upper Mississippi squadrons—besides cutting off Port Hudson by water.

On July the fourth Vicksburg surrendered to Grant. Port Hudson, starving and besieged by Banks with his army of twenty thousand men—as well as by the continual two-month bombardment by Farragut's fleet—surrendered a few days later. By midsummer, 1863, the merchant steamer *Imperial*, from St. Louis, arrived at New Orleans—which meant that the river was at last open to navigation throughout its course. On August the first Farragut went aboard the *Hartford* to the ringing of church bells and the echoing cheers from his fleet, homeward bound. Nine days later he was in New York, after eighteen months of the hardest service of his fifty-two years in the Navy.

18

Mobile Bay at Last

Two years earlier Farragut had come with his family to New York, an unknown Southern naval officer under suspicion. Now as the *Hartford* steamed into New York harbor the pier was crowded with a seething mass of people, shouting themselves hoarse to welcome him as the "Hero of the Gulf." Feeling old and tired, he had come for a rest; but he got little of that. He wrote to Bell in the Gulf: "I am run to death with the attention of good people, but I am beginning to give out; as I am not able to bear my honors."

He was eager to get back and continue his naval campaign, but the *Hartford* needed extensive repairs; for during her nineteen months of active service she had been struck two hundred and forty-nine times by shot and shell. It took five months of refitting, repairing, and replacing of the crew before she was finally ready for active duty again. Farragut found many new faces aboard, but they all beamed when, in spite of a northeast blizzard, he put out to sea on January the fifth. Nine days later they were in Pensacola, exchanging cold and snow for heat and mosquitoes!

Once there he found everybody suffering from "ram fever," the Union officers warning one another of the ironclads being built above Mobile. These Mobile rams were to attack and break through the blockading vessels, proceed up the Mississippi, re-take New Orleans with the help of troops in Louisiana and Mississippi and of gunboats in the Red River. Confederate leader Buchanan, at Fort Morgan, was supposed to attack with his ram Tennessee in March.

In the two years since Farragut had conquered New Orleans and had been prevented from going on to take Mobile, the latter had developed rapidly as a center of commerce for the Confederacy. Despite an alert blockade, runners passed in and out continuously. River-system facilities for inland transportation, the railroads of the back country, and the manufacturing interests of the town had steadily increased. Since Fort Morgan was on a point commanding Mobile, troops would be needed to isolate it from the mainland while Union ships were holding the bay. In 1864 Mobile would be much more difficult to take than when he had first planned it in 1862.

For six months Farragut rocked and sizzled on the waves of the Gulf, crying for troops and monitors. "If Porter would only send me two ironclads!" he wrote to his son again and again. Meanwhile he was busy checking his fleet, to have everything ready when "the world turns round and it comes my turn to do something, and then I will 'pitch in.' " That was part of his greatness—his ability to wait during heartbreaking delays and then, when the time did come, to take hold with a masterful will. During this time he tightened the blockade and caught ten runners, while four others were destroyed.

He knew, too, that the eyes of the country were upon him, wondering at his long delay and impatient for another victory. His wife sent him clippings from enthusiastic editors who wrote: "Let him take Mobile, and then Charleston, and then let's make him President." To this he answered: "If I survived those two engagements, then surely a Presidential campaign would finish me."

In April he wrote his son from New Orleans, where he was still organizing his forces: "I write flat on my back. I am just getting over a boil that would humble the greatest hero that ever fought a Ram." Throughout this period he suffered so much from boils that at times he could not walk, sit, or stand except in the greatest agony, yet he could joke about it to his son.

While bad news of defeats to troops in the West and the near-disastrous result of the Red River expeditions came to him, Farragut was cheered by one incident. In mid-June the Union League Club of New York sent him a sword with this message: "As a slight token of the high esteem in which you are held here by all, and an evidence of our appreciation of the brilliant services you have rendered to our country." It was a beautiful blade sheathed in a scabbard of massive silver and gold, and had a hilt with Farragut's initials set in diamonds.

No public demonstration on land could be made for him, since Farragut with his blockade was "literally watching his enemies who like hawks are ready to pounce upon us at the first unguarded moment." But as usual he shared his honors with his men. Calling his orderly to take the sword to the enlisted men, he said, "Let them see it. Tell them from me that they helped me earn it."

Though he wrote continually to Washington asking for troops, ships, and supplies, they did not arrive and he feared each delay meant the enemy would be stronger to receive him.

When Buchanan finally ran his Confederate *Tennessee* into the bay, the tide had fallen so much that she was left aground. The failure of this surprise attack brought some hope to Farragut, and it frightened Secretary Welles into ordering the monitor *Manhattan*, at New York, to join Farragut.

Unexpected setbacks in the West and bloody repulses for Grant in Virginia added to Farragut's anxiety. Yet he could write to his wife: "Now you know *Grant cannot* make his men fight if they are not so disposed and all his courage and strategy amount to nothing; remember, my darling, these lines. *Victory or success is with God.* . . . He must give Grant that Power over his officers and men to fight and himself the gift of foresight into results and the daring to undertake. Now as I believe God is on our side, I think He will sooner or later give us the proper instrument to carry us through the fiery furnace."

Finally, toward the end of July, the monitors began to arrive, together with the troops needed to invest the forts. August the fourth was set for the attack, even though the *Richmond* and one monitor, the *Tecumseh*, were still fueling at Pensacola. Then, though they arrived in time, one whole squadron had to be left behind because yellow fever struck the men. Farragut was sad that its commander, Rear Admiral Bailey, who had been with him at the taking of New Orleans, also was sick.

Once again the Admiral had no sea for maneuvering, and had to take his fleet into a landlocked bay defended by three forts, naval units, and a new device—submerged mines—called torpedoes. Of the three forts—Morgan, Gaines, and Powell—the first was the strongest, commanding the main channel into the bay.

South and east of Fort Gaines the Confederates had driven great quantities of piles through the shallow water of the flats to keep smaller gunboats out. From the end of these piles two lines of submerged mines ran toward Fort Morgan, ending at a red buoy. Between this and the fort was a channel used by blockade runners, but now cut off by obstructions. Since this channel ran so close to Fort Morgan, any vessel passing through it would be an easy target for the Confederate batteries.

The week before, Farragut had sent his aide, Lieutenant John C. Watson, at night in a cutter with muffled oars, to cut an opening through these obstructions. As usual, Farragut walked the deck anxiously, praying that his men come back safely. By working all night through three nights, Watson and his men succeeded in making an opening wide enough for the fleet to go through.

In the bay the Confederates had three wooden gunboats with the ram *Tennessee* and, compared with Farragut's four rams and thirteen other ships, this was not much of a force. But the enemy was in position to rake the oncoming Union fleet as it filed through the channel, while Farragut could only reply with a few bow guns from his leading ship. The formidable *Tennessee*, with her iron prow for ramming an enemy under the water line, could inflict tremendous damage to the Union wooden ships.

Two weeks before, the Admiral's orders had been to all vessels to clear for battle, stripping away all unnecessary spars and rigging. On the starboard side, facing Fort Morgan, he had splinter nettings stretched; for, thrown about by a striking shot, splinters could be as deadly as an exploding shell.

Round the wheel on each ship a high barricade of sails, hammocks, and the like was placed, protecting the helmsmen. On decks, over machinery, bulky materials such as sandbags, piles of canvas, and spare anchor chains were banked to keep out plunging shot. Overlapping chain cables, spread along the side of each ship, made a coat of mail for the engine room. All small boats on the starboard side were removed, while those on the port side were lowered to the water's edge to keep them out of harm's way and yet have them ready for any emergency. As before his other two great victories, Farragut paid attention to detail and showed concern for the protection of his men.

And, as in passing Port Hudson, gunboats were lashed to the large wooden ships, on the sides away from the fort. As usual, since he believed that "exposure is one of the penalties of rank in the Navy," Farragut wanted to lead the column. But his officers persuaded him to let the *Brooklyn* do so, because, they urged, "She has four bow guns, an advantage when heading directly into the enemy flotilla." Besides, affixed to her jib-boom, she had an ingenious arrangement for picking up torpedoes.

At three in the morning on August the fifth Farragut sent his steward to investigate the weather. He reported, "Cloudy but wind is southwest, sir."

"Fine," said Farragut. "It will blow the smoke directly into the eyes of the gunners at Fort Morgan."

A sailor pointed to a comet flash across the heavens toward the northeast. "Another omen of victory," Farragut said. By five-thirty, with four rams to the starboard, the *Tecumseh* ahead and the *Brooklyn* leading the wooden ships, Farragut on the *Hartford* following, the fleet was moving in a northerly course toward the entrance to the bay.

As the *Brooklyn* and the *Tecumseh* came within range, both sides began firing. On the *Hartford*, Fleet Captain Drayton stood on the poop deck with his aides about him, while three veteran sailors who had been with Farragut in every battle stood proudly at the wheel. Above in the mizzen the pilot stood near the speaking trumpet to call directions to the helmsmen; and as the smoke rolled higher, Farragut climbed farther up in the port main rigging for a better view of what was going on. Fearing that his Admiral might be wounded and hurled to the deck or thrown into the sea, Captain Drayton sent Quartermaster Knowles with a lead line to secure him to the rigging. Though Farragut objected, "Never mind; I'm all right," Knowles went ahead lashing him to the mast. Within calling distance, made fast to the starboard wheelhouse of the Metacomet, was Captain Jouett, with whom the Admiral could communicate easily.

For two hours the Confederates pounded the leading ships—concentrating their fire on the flagship Hartford, which took an assault that shook her from stem to stern. Once a one-hundred-and-twenty-pound shot from the Tennessee struck her mainmast, nearly cutting it in two. Great splinters, some as big as logs, slammed across the deck in spite of the nettings. Men were killed and wounded on all sides, the decks running red and slippery with their blood; and for twenty minutes both the Confederate vessels and Fort Morgan focused their fire on the Hartford.

Meanwhile the leading monitor, Tecumseh, had forged past Fort Morgan, her turret guns firing steadily since the beginning of the action. Suddenly the Brooklyn, using Army signaling instead of Navy, confused the line by slowing up to await orders in answer to her signals. The Tecumseh was puzzled and instead of obeying Farragut's order—"Stay inside the buoys"—thought it a mistake and turned to the port side. Scarcely had she passed the invisible lines of torpedoes when a muffled roar sounded and a great jet of water shot beneath the bow. An instant later she pitched down by the bow; her stern rose until her wheel was seen whirling in the air; then, while a score of men leaped from her deck and turret, under she went, with Captain Craven going down with his ship.

Immediately Farragut ordered a boat from the Union Metacomet, under Nields, to go to the rescue. When General Page in Fort Morgan saw the boat on its errand of mercy, he said, "Pass the order not to fire on that craft; she is saving drowning men."

On the Confederate *Tennessee*, only one hundred yards away, the enemy crew, gazing at the immense bubbles of steam issuing from the *Tecumseh*, spoke only in whispers and held their fire. Just twenty-one of the one hundred and fourteen officers and men on the *Tecumseh* escaped death.

From his high post Farragut had watched with horror the almost instant sinking of the monitor. He had seen the *Brooklyn* come to a stop. Its captain, frightened by this sinking, became panicky when he saw floating empty shell cases and, thinking they were torpedoes, backed his engines and almost collided with the *Hartford*.

Meanwhile the vessels in the rear were pressing on and a flooding tide was sweeping all together. The *Brooklyn* swung across the channel and blocked the way, and in the confusion the Union ships slackened their fire while the guns from Fort Morgan increased theirs in rapidity and effectiveness.

"What's the trouble?" Farragut signaled to Alden on the *Brooklyn*.

"Torpedoes!" was the answer.

Disaster was imminent and, knowing the risk which must be taken if the whole fleet were not to be caught hopelessly under the guns of the fort and the flotilla, Farragut shouted his historic words: "Damn the torpedoes! Drayton, Jouett! Full speed ahead!"

Quickly he placed his *Hartford* on her new course, passing the hesitant *Brooklyn* to the left and steaming right through the danger area into the lead. The officers on the other vessels followed, believing they were going to a "noble death with their commander in chief."

But no explosion rocked the *Hartford*! The flagship forged on, and before the fleet could straighten out she was pushing on alone about a mile ahead—beyond the range of Fort Morgan guns. Immediately the Confederate *Tennessee* attacked, trying to ram her; but the *Hartford*, speedier and more maneuverable, poured broadsides into the ram and advanced on the three wooden gunboats.

Now the rest of the Union fleet was coming up; and as each ship passed the *Tennessee* it poured shot into her and passed on to join Farragut, who anchored four miles northeast of Fort Morgan. The Admiral's heart swelled with pride as each of his vessels passed the *Hartford* with flags flying and his sailors cheering and waving to him. When the last of the Union ships had fought her way through the bay, the Rebel *Tennessee* withdrew under the protective fire of the guns of Fort Morgan, and the Southern gunboats fled. So finished the first two hours of bloody fighting.

Farragut's entire fleet had taken a severe battering, especially his own ship. A single Confederate shell had killed ten and wounded five, while the masts and sides of the *Hartford* were pierced with great holes where shells had found their mark. While his crews on the heavy ships set to work clearing away the wreckage of the battle, Farragut was making a new plan. Captain Drayton said to him, "What we have done has been well done, sir; but it counts for nothing so long as the *Tennessee* is there under the guns of Fort Morgan."

"I know it," said Farragut, "and as soon as it is dark enough for the smoke to prevent them from distinguishing friend from foe, I intend to go in with the three monitors, myself on board the *Manahattan*."

At that very moment Admiral Buchanan, senior naval officer of the Confederacy, was ordering the commanding officer of the *Tennessee*, "Follow them, Johnston; we can't let them off this way." He and Farragut had been good friends years before in the Navy, but now they were bitter enemies. Earlier, when Buchanan had seen the *Hartford* isolated at the head of the column he had ordered the ram to attack—hoping to sink her with the iron beak. But Farragut had been too quick for him, and now he was determined to get the Union Admiral while the latter's crews were tired and his own still fresh.

So Farragut was suprised when he saw the enemy *Tennessee* coming out from under the protection of the fort, heading directly for the *Hartford*. "Old Buck's coming out!" he cried. "Drayton, we must signal 'Get under way at once.' We must be ready for him." Then he sent another signal to all ships: "Attack the ram, not only with guns but with bows on at full speed!"

The *Monongahela* was the first to attack the rebel, attempting to run her down, but succeeded in striking only a glancing blow —and received two shells in her berth deck, seriously damaging the vessel.

Next the *Lackwanna* struck at full speed at right angles near the afterend of the casemate, crashing her own bow without more than a jolt to the ram.

Then came the *Hartford's* turn to slam at the ironclad, and the two vessels slid grinding alongside each other. Farragut started to jump into the port mizzen rigging above the poop deck to see the effect of the ramming, and Lieutenant Watson tried to seize his coat to hold him back. Grabbing a rope end, Watson climbed up after the Admiral, saying, "Sir, if you *will* stand there, you had better secure yourself against falling."

The Admiral laughed but took a turn around and over the shrouds and his body, while Watson stood near him with a drawn revolver ready to shoot anybody on the ram who might attempt to pick off his commanding officer.

Farragut was only a few feet above the ram as the port sides of the two vessels rasped each other and their guns, almost touching, exchanged broadsides. One shell entered the *Hartford* and exploded, killing and wounding a number of men.

Then the *Hartford* stood off to get up momentum to override the ram, but the rebel *Lackawanna* crashed into her a little forward of the mizzenmast and cut her down to within two feet of the water. Farragut had descended from the rigging and was standing aft in the poop deck. Instantly he climbed over the side to examine the damage.

The men, alarmed that the ship was sinking, shouted, "Save the Admiral! Get the Admiral out of the ship!" Hearing them, Farragut's heart warmed to think of the men's concern first for him, not for themselves. When he found the flagship still would float, he ordered another try at the *Tennessee*.

Meanwhile the Union monitors had been firing at the ram with their powerful guns whenever they could without hitting one of their own ships. The *Manhattan* succeeded in planting a shot that crashed the armor of the rebel *Tennessee*, which, with the repeated hammering of the guns from the monitors, had its exposed rudder chains shot away so it could not steer a course. Soon her smokestack was blasted off and her gunports on her port side were so jammed by the blows of heavy shot that they would not open. Then like a water-logged derelict she drifted, unable to bring a single gun to bear while the ring of Union ships blazed away at her.

As the *Hartford* again came surging up to attack, a white flag appeared on the *Tennessee*. So ended the second stage of the Battle of Mobile Bay. The *Winnebago* towed the *Tennessee* up to anchorage near the *Hartford*; and later the *Bienville* took her to New Orleans, where a board estimated her value at $883,880!

Hearing that Buchanan's leg had been broken during the action, Farragut sent his surgeon aboard to attend him; but Dr. Palmer was rudely received. "I don't pretend to be a friend of Farragut, " snapped Buchanan. "I am a Southern man, an enemy and a rebel." The doctor, realizing that his own presence would only cause trouble, withdrew. Later he suggested to Farragut that another vessel take all wounded, both Union and Confederate, to Pensacola, which the *Metacomet* did.

Union losses were heavy: fifty-two killed and one hundred and seventy wounded—with twenty-five killed and twenty-eight wounded on the *Hartford* alone, which had been hit twenty times with five shells puncturing the hull. The Confederate casualty list was only twelve killed and twenty wounded, but many were taken prisoner.

In its entire history the *Hartford* was hit two hundred and sixty-four times, yet Admiral Farragut never suffered a scratch. Once again he wrote to his wife: "Though I am worn out with mental strain and physical fatigue, I escaped—thank God—without a scratch."

In his report to Secretary Welles, Farragut expressed particularly generous praise and appreciation for his subordinates. To the men in his fleet he sent a general order next day, commending them for their gallant conduct, their courageous performance and cheerfulness, and expressing "thanks for their noble and implicit confidence in their leader."

So the battle was won, and Mobile was back under the Stars and Stripes. The South's most powerful ironclad was captured, her commanding officer, the ranking one of the Confederate Navy, a prisoner of war. Blockade runners could no longer slip out on dark nights with their cargoes of cotton and dash back with rifles and cannon from England.

For Farragut this was his hardest and his greatest achievement; by his daring and quick decision he had snatched victory from what seemed certain catastrophe. And here he had given the Navy its most stirring slogan: *"Full speed ahead!"*

19

The Last Cruise

I N every American journal Farragut read praise of his deeds, and poets especially were inspired. One composition in the *Army and Navy Journal* stressed what his men felt about him:

> But Farragut is leading us
> And we will clear the way.

Another, in *Harper's Weekly*, celebrated the Battle of Mobile Bay in:

> Oh, never through all time shall be forgot
> His last brave deed, now told on every lip,
> When on he sailed, amid a storm of shot,
> Lashed in the rigging of his staunch old ship.

But on board the *Hartford* had been a paymaster poet, William T. Meredith, serving as secretary to the Admiral. His poem entitled "Farragut" became so popular that it was memorized and

152

recited by two generations of Yankee schoolboys after the war. It reveals the devotion, amounting to worship, which the Admiral's officers and men felt for him. The last verse was his favorite:

> Oh! while Atlantic's breast
> Bears a white sail,
> While the Gulf's towering crest
> Tops a green vale,
> Men thy bold deeds shall tell,
> Old Heart of Oak,
> Daring Dave Farragut,
> Thunderbolt stroke!

But Farragut's head was not swelled by such flattery. What his former teacher, Charles Folsom, wrote of him at this time was true: "The better his countrymen understand him, the more they will see that his is no false brilliancy; that he is not a flashing meteor, but a star in our national firmament."

After taking Fort Gaines and Fort Powell with the aid of troops, he wrote his wife: "I know that few men could have gone through what I have in the last three years, and no one will ever know except yourself perhaps. What the fight was to my poor brains, neither you nor any one else will ever be able to comprehend."

Several times he fainted away while talking to his officers, because his mind had been "constantly on the stretch" for months. "This blockade duty with eighty vessels, nearly a thousand miles of coast to defend, with 185 harbor and river openings in the Confederate coastline to watch day and night, has been a terrible pull upon my brain," he wrote Rear Admiral Davis. Finally he wrote Secretary Welles: "I have now been down in this Gulf and the Caribbean Sea nearly five years out of six, except for the short visit home last fall, and the last six months have been such a severe drag upon me that I must rest if it is to be had."

The Secretary answered that he turn over his command to

whomever he saw fit and return home. It was then that Commodore Palmer took over the Western Gulf Squadron, and December, 1864, saw the *Hartford* steaming up the narrows of New York harbor.

Though his wife had warned him to be prepared for an enthusiastic welcome when he arrived in New York, he expected nothing like the demonstration at the Battery. Cheer after cheer arose as he stepped off the pier. *"Daring Dave Farragut!"* they called to him as hundreds pressed forward to shake his hand before he could get into his waiting coach. During the drive to the Custom House the crowds followed in the streets, reaching out to touch him and salute him, shouting "Little Admiral!"

At the Custom House he listened to speeches, cheers, and even a poem read in his honor. There the Merchants' Association presented him with a gift of fifty thousand dollars to buy a home in New York City. "This," he said, smiling and waving the check at them, "I would be glad to do."

By Christmas, 1864, Congress had created the rank of Vice Admiral to confer upon Farragut. Not until January, 1865, did he see his wife and son in their home at Hastings-on-Hudson. Here, too, the villagers went wild with excitement over their returning hero. Triumphal arches decorated with evergreens and flags, others painted with the names of his victories, reached over the streets, heralding their welcome. Over the doorway to his home they had placed in evergreen letters the name "Virginia L. Farragut," which pleased him more than all the recognition he had received. He now rested for two months at home, renewing his strength.

Later he was at Richmond, after the evacuation of that city, exclaiming, "Thank God, it's over!" He and his wife went to Norfolk to see relatives, but the cold shoulder turned on them by old friends cut short that visit.

In July, 1866, Congress created the new rank of Admiral for Farragut, with a yearly salary of ten thousand dollars, and bestowed it on him the next day. He thus became the first Admiral of the United States Navy, an office "created to reward extraordinary services to the nation, not to be filled by promotion, but by men who had in like manner earned such a reward."

In May, 1867, Farragut received orders for the last cruise of his career. He was to be gone a year and a half in command of the European Squadron. Mrs. Farragut was to follow him by passenger steamer from port to port, but at the last minute President Johnson telegraphed orders permitting Mrs. Farragut to accompany the Admiral on the flagship. Mrs. Pennock, wife of Flag Captain Alexander Pennock and Mrs. Farragut's cousin, was allowed to go also.

As his flag was hoisted on the *Franklin* late in June, Farragut remarked, "This is the first four-starred Admiral's flag to float over an American man-of-war." She was a steam frigate, manned by a crew of seven hundred and fifty men; but out on the broad Atlantic, Farragut hoisted the propeller and once more enjoyed seeing his ship under sail.

The *Franklin* made the round of European countries—France, England, Sweden, Russia, Italy, and Spain. The Admiral was received by Napoleon III, Queen Victoria, kings and emperors, important personages in armies and navies and in the political world all over Europe. He made the round of salutes, receptions, balls, dinners, and official occasions of all sorts, returning the honor with magnificent balls aboard the *Franklin*. All these attentions had a political significance, for he impressed the nations of Europe with the idea that peace with the United States was desirable.

In his diary he did not forget to make note of matters that might be useful to his government in time of war. He inspected docks, arsenals, ships; he recorded the position and strength of forts, the novel features of ships, the relative power of a fifteen-inch Dahlgren and a nine-inch rifle tested in England. This work he enjoyed more than all the entertainment by royalty.

However, one reception particularly pleased him—that accorded him at Ciudadella on the island of Minorca, the original home of his father. Landing at Port Mahan the day after Christmas, he found the people of the island gathered in great throngs along the route of his journey. The alcalde and other officials of Ciudadella met him four miles from the city's limits, bade him welcome, and escorted him to the town of his ancestors. Here he was transferred from his closed carriage to an open barouche so everyone could see him. Streets, housetops, walls, balconies were crowded with people, filling the air with cheers as he waved to them and answered them in their own tongue.

After being escorted to places of interest about the city, he was lodged at the house of a distinguished citizen. There the town council came in a body to present him with a book containing the register of his father's baptism, and also with a copy of a law passed that day making him a citizen of Ciudadella.

That evening a banquet was given in his honor at the palace of the Marquis de Albranca. The principal ornament of the table was a large centerpiece representing the castle of Ciudadella, on the four walls of which was written "Homenage de Respeco y Patriotismo Ciudadella." From the center of this castle rose a column of victory bearing the inscription "El Gran Almirante Farragut," and on top of it was a small statuette of Fame blowing a trumpet. The whole was decorated with red, white, and blue ribbons. This was given to Mrs. Farragut afterward, and cherished as a souvenir of the remarkable visit. Next morning as the Farraguts left, the roads were once more thronged with an enthusiastic populace escorting the Admiral to his ship.

With the sounds of Spanish all around him he recalled a scene
sixty years earlier when, as a boy of six, he listened to his mother
singing a Spanish song. It told of the exploits of one Don Pedro
Farragut, ancestor of his father, who strummed a guitar as his
wife sang. For a moment he was back with his brother William
and his sister Nancy sitting in the log cabin at Stony Point.

When Farragut anchored off the Battery on November 10,
1868, and hauled down his flag, his European cruise of seventeen
months came to a close.

Once again, when he came home, prominent politicians begged
Farragut to run in the National Democratic Convention to be
held that year—as a candidate for the Presidency of the United
States. But he wrote in reply: "My entire life has been spent in
the Navy; by a steady perserverance and devotion to it, I have
been favored with success in my profession, and to risk that reputation by entering a new career at my advanced age, and that
career one of which I have little or no knowledge, is more than
any one has a right to expect of me."

In the summer of 1869 Admiral and Mrs. Farragut revisited
the Pacific Coast and the navy yard that he had set up years before
at Mare Island. A large cavalcade of citizens of Vallejo came to
meet them and escort them to the town for a reception. Some of
the men who had worked for him fifteen years before said, "You
left us a captain. You are here today the High Admiral of the
Navy."

Greatly moved by these old friends about him, Farragut said,
"I've only done my duty. The will of the Almighty is seen in the
result. I'm happy to spend with my family some short time among
you, and get a good rest." That evening he was entertained with
fireworks and a torchlight procession.

On the way home, in Chicago, Farragut suffered a heart attack, and for a few days his life was despaired of. But with skillful treatment and good nursing he was able to resume his journey.

During that winter he had several more attacks, but his powerful constitution helped him recover from them. His last official duty was to take charge of the naval obsequies for George Peabody, when the remains arrived at Portland, Maine, in January, 1870.

As the Admiral's health continued gradually but surely to fail, the doctor suggested he leave New York during the summer. He decided to pay a visit to the Pennocks in Portsmouth, New Hampshire, where Commodore Pennock was Commandant of the navy yard. The Navy Department placed at his disposal the dispatch steamer *Tallapoosa*. On July the fourth, as the vessel entered Portsmouth harbor, he heard the guns booming in salute to him. He left his sickbed, dressed himself in full uniform, and went on deck. There, as he gazed at his blue flag flying at the masthead, he said sadly, "It would be well if I died *now*, in harness."

A few days later, while wandering around the Portsmouth Navy Yard, he went aboard the old sailing sloop of war *Dale*, then lying dismantled at the wharf. Looking about the vessel whose work, like his, was finished, he said to the old sailor who was her caretaker, "This is the last time I shall ever tread the deck of a man-of-war."

A few days later he was too ill to leave his bed. With him, on August 14, 1870, were his wife and son, members of the Pennock family, three physicians, and comrades in arms.

And just as eight bells struck, the spirit of the Great Admiral put out to sea. David Farragut was embarked on his last, eternal cruise.

20

Fighting Farragut

ADMIRAL FARRAGUT's life can well be an inspiration to the youth of today. He never had the advantages of going to school for more than a few months at a time, but, eager to learn, he welcomed everyone who could teach him something. He learned in the school of experience, and could speak French, Spanish, Italian, and even Arabic fluently. When his eyes were weakened by sunstroke he had his junior officers read to him every day, his favorite books being the Bible, Shakespeare, and James Fenimore Cooper's tales.

Wherever he went, he talked with the people he met in order to enlarge his information on professional, scientific, and political subjects. And he was up-to-date on everything new in guns and ships.

Farragut readily adapted himself to new conditions, no matter how difficult, and to new weapons. The problems he had to meet in the Civil War included conditions he did not like. He hated river and harbor fighting, and he had had no experience with ironclads or mines. Yet, since all his life he believed in "full speed ahead," out of these new elements he forged victories. But he left nothing to chance; he studied his job and, when the time came for action, he made his decisions and followed them through to bold triumph. As he said, "I fix my eyes on my object, ready to tread down or fight through any obstacles in the path I see fit to follow. I will attack, regardless of consequences, and never turn back."

With his dash and daring and his dogged idea that the enemy must be met wherever he is, plus his intuitive knowledge of the enemy's weak points, he has been compared most often with Lord Nelson. But Farragut's private life and high ideals set him above his English compeer.

More than any other naval officer, he inspired personal devotion in his officers and men. They admired his skill and courage, loved him for his interest in their welfare and happiness, and knew he was fair and just. When he recommended someone for promotion and was told the officer was too young, he answered, "Well, if he can't stand prosperity, that will be his own fault." Remembering his own long wait for promotion, he said, "No man can tell how he will act in a responsible position till he finds himself in it."

Farragut's life shows that success is no accident. He proved that the surest way to become great is by thoroughly mastering the duties of each grade if one wants to rise to the top of his profession. When fame came to him he could brush it aside, because his mind was fixed on the full development of his powers to carry out effectively his particular job.

His whole life was a preparation for the brilliant victories won in a total of less than *six hours* of actual fighting! He became the first Admiral of our Navy because he lived what he had taught his men: *"Don't be afraid of doing too much; those who are, seldom do as much as they ought."*

Commodore George Dewey, who served under Farragut as a junior officer throughout the Civil War, writing to Loyall Farragut after his own victory in Manila Bay in 1898, said: "In all my operations in the Philippines, the example of the Greatest Admiral, your father, was constantly before me. In great emergencies, I always said to myself, 'What would Farragut have done under like emergencies?' As I entered Manila Bay I felt sure I was doing exactly as he would have done."

Gentle and kind by nature, he was fierce, brave, and resourceful in war; and as "Fighting Farragut" he lives in the hearts of men today.

Chronology

1801

July 5   James Glasgow Farragut was born at Campbell's Station, near Knoxville, Tennessee.

1810

December 17   Appointed midshipman in the United States Navy. Name of David given him.

1811

August   Sailed on first cruise.

1812

June   Sailed from New York on second cruise after declaration of war.

1813

June 30   Put in command of the *Alexander Barclay* as Prize Master.

1814

March 28   His first battle on the *Essex* against the *Phoebe* and the *Cherub*.

July 7   Arrived at New York, a paroled prisoner.

November 30   Exchanged for British prisoner.

1815

April   Sailed from Boston for the Mediterranean on the ship of the line *Independence*, returning in the fall of the same year.

1816

Spring   Sailed from Boston for the Mediterranean a second time; wintered at Port Mahon, his father's birthplace.

1817

Spring   Began an extended cruise in the Mediterranean.

1818

January   Remained in Tunis with United States Consul and teacher, Charles Folsom; learned French, Italian, Spanish, and Arabic.

December   Reported for duty on board the *Franklin* at Messina, Sicily.

1819

Spring   Continued his cruise in the Mediterranean. First promotion—appointed acting lieutenant on board the little brig *Spark*.

1820

November 20   Arrived at New York to undergo his examinations; failed.

1821

July   Passed examinations for lieutenancy.

1822

May   Went to sea on the *John Adams*.

December   Returned to Norfolk.

1823

February   Sailed on the schooner *Greyhound* for the West Indies. Became executive officer of the *Sea Gull*.

1824

July   Given command of the *Ferret*; treated and saved crew from yellow fever.

September   Married Miss Susan C. Marchant of Norfolk.

1825

January 23   Commissioned Lieutenant. Chosen for *Brandywine*, new frigate escorting Lafayette back to France.

1826

May   Arrived in New York.

October   Ordered to the receiving ship *Alert* at Norfolk.

1828

October   Ordered to the *Vandalia*.

December   Sailed for Brazil Station.

1830

February   Arrived back at Norfolk.

1832

December   Ordered to Natchez.

1833

January   Ordered to Charleston because of the nullification controversy.

May   Sailed for coast of Brazil.

1834

June   Commanded *Boxer* at Rio de Janeiro.

1838

August   Commanded the sloop *Erie* in Mexican waters.

December   Witnessed the capture of San Juan d'Ulloa by the French.

1840

December 20   Mrs. Farragut died after a sixteen-year illness, which in the past two years had necessitated his taking leaves to care for her at Norfolk.

1841

February   Became executive officer of the *Delaware*.

September 9   Commissioned Commander.

1842

June   Sailed for the South American station. Put in command of the *Decatur*.

1843

December 26)   Married Miss Virginia Loyall of Norfolk.

1844

April   Ordered to the receiving ship *Pennsylvania*.

July   Ordered to navy yard at Norfolk.

October 12 \   Only son, Loyall, born.

1847

February   Commanded the *Saratoga* ordered to Vera Cruz. All men aboard stricken with yellow fever.

1848

February 19   Arrived at New York. Ordered to navy yard at Norfolk.

1850–51

                Stationed in Washington and Norfolk. Compiled book of ordnance regulations.

1854

June   Ordered to California to establish a navy yard at Mare Island. His wife and son lived here with him until 1858.

1855

September \   Commissioned as Captain.

1859

January	Commanded sloop of war *Brooklyn*.
March	Escorted Robert McLane, new American minister, to Mexico.

1861

April	Forced to leave Norfolk at the time of Virginia's secession from the Union. After fifty-two years in the Navy, moved to Hastings-on-the-Hudson.
December	Appointed flag officer of the new warship *Hartford*.

1862

January	Given command of Western Gulf Squadron; sent to New Orleans.
April 24	Became "Hero of New Orleans." Passed forts at New Orleans—opening up the Mississippi for the Union, which might now be saved.
June	Farragut passed batteries of the Gibraltar of the West—Vicksburg. Freed Mississippi for Union armies and ships.
July 16	Commissioned Rear Admiral—a grade created for him—first Admiral of the Navy. Maintained blockade at the mouth of the Mississippi.

1863

March 14	Passed the batteries at Port Hudson.
August	On short furlough home.

1864

January	Sailed for Gulf to prepare for attack on Mobile Bay.
August 5	Attacked and captured Mobile.
December 23	Commissioned Vice Admiral, a title created for him. Returned to New York, whose citizens gave him $50,000 for a home in New York.

1866

July 26　　　Commissioned Admiral, first full Admiral of the Navy.

1867

June 28　　　Given the squadron frigate *Franklin*—special permission granted to his wife to accompany him—on good will tour to European countries.

1869

Summer　　　Revisited Mare Island to see men who worked under him in 1854. Suffered heart attack on way home.

1870

August 14　　Died at Portsmouth, New Hampshire.

September 30 Public funeral and burial in Woodlawn Cemetery in New York City.

Bibliography

BOOKS

Barnes, James, *Midshipman Farragut.* D. Appleton & Co., New York, 1909.

Bolton, Sarah K., *Lives of Poor Boys Who Became Famous.* Thomas Y. Crowell, New York, 1937.

Chavanne, R. N., *David Farragut, Midshipman.* Coward-McCann, New York, 1941.

Dictionary of American Biography. Vol. 6, Chas. Scribner's Sons, New York, 1931. Article by Charles O. Paullin.

Farragut, Loyall, *The Life of David Glasgow Farragut, First Admiral of the United States Navy (embodying his Journal and Letters).* D. Appleton & Co., New York, 1879.

Frothingham, Jessie Peabody, *Sea Fighters from Drake to Farragut.* Chas. Scribner's Sons, New York, 1892.

Headley, Joel T., *Farragut and Our Naval Commanders.* E. B. Treat, 771 Broadway, New York, 1880.

Headley, Phineas Camp, *Life and Naval Career of Vice-Admiral David Glasgow Farragut.* Wm. H. Appleton, New York, 1865.

Lewis, Charles Lee, *David Glasgow Farragut.* U. S. Naval Institute, Annapolis, Maryland. Vol. I, *Admiral in the Making,* 1941. Vol. II, *Our First Admiral,* 1942.

Mahan, Alfred Thayer, *Admiral Farragut* (Great Commander Series). Appleton, New York, 1897.

169

Montgomery, James E., *Our Admiral's Flag Abroad: The Cruise of the Franklin.* G. P. Putnam & Son, New York, 1869.

Porter, David, *Journal of the Cruise of the* Essex. Bradford & Inskeep, Philadelphia, 1815. 2nd edition revised by Wiley & Halsted, New York, 1822.

Spears, John Randolph, *David G. Farragut* (American Crisis Biographies), George W. Jacobs, Philadelphia, 1905.

Stevens, William O., *David Glasgow Farragut, Our First Admiral.* Dodd, Mead, New York, 1942.

Note: The two-volume biography by Charles Lee Lewis, scholar and Professor of History and English at the U.S. Naval Academy at Annapolis, is the latest and most thorough. He has discovered documents, letters, journals, papers and original logbooks, etc., which even Farragut's son, Loyall, never had access to. Also he found the original manuscript of Admiral Farragut's *Some Reminiscences of Early Life* by D. G. Farragut, Captain the U.S. Navy.

MAGAZINES AND NEWSPAPERS

American Historical Magazine and Tennessee Historical Society Quarterly, Vols. II & III, Nashville, Tenn. (These are combined as one magazine now.)

Chicago *Daily Tribune*, article. "Controversy Grows over Admiral Farragut's Flagship." Chicago, Ill. August 27, 1952.

Christian Science Monitor, article. "Farragut's Flagship Poses Million Dollar Test for Navy." Boston, Mass. March 12, 1951.

Harper's New Monthly Magazine, article. "Cruise of the *Essex*." New York, August, 1859.

Knoxville Sentinel, article. "Farragut's Beginnings" by George P. Mellon, Knoxville, Tenn. April 9, 1910.

Louisiana Historical Quarterly, article. "Father of Admiral Farragut" by Charles O. Paullin. New Orleans, La. January, 1930.

Portsmouth *Daily Evening Times*. Portsmouth, N. H. July and August issues, 1870 (in Portsmouth, N. H. Library).

Saint Nicholas Magazine, article. "Little David" by Don. G. Seitz. New York, July, 1924.

(For pictures of this period see *Room to Swing a Cat* by Lieutenant Fredrick J. Bell, U.S. Navy. Longmans, Green & Co., Toronto & New York, 1938.

and *Photographs of the Civil War* by Mathew B. Brady from private collection of Edward Bailey Easton, Hartford, Connecticut, 1907.)

(For Paintings, Relics and Ship Models see the exhibits at the New York Historical Society building and the marine rooms at the Museum of the City of New York.)

Index